CAN I PEE IN YOUR HELMET?

CAN I PEE IN YOUR HELMET?

Riotous policing tales from 1980s Britain

Brian Mitchell

The moral right of Brian Mitchell to be identified as the author of this work has been asserted under the Copyright, Designs and Patents Act 1998.

All rights reserved. No part of this publication may be reproduced or transmitted in any form or by any means, electronic or mechanical, including photocopy, recording, or any information storage and retrieval system, without permission in writing from the author.

This book recounts real events. Names, characters and their backstories are used fictitiously unless stated otherwise.

ISBN 9781836543497

Cover design by Laura Mitchell

Dedication

A few characters from my days on "Green Section" who are, sadly, no longer with us.

In fond remembrance of Jeff Whitcome, Brian Lunt, Diane Berkley, Kenneth Gordon Hobbs and Rodney Hoare.

Acknowledgements

Thanks to Laura Mitchell, Stuart Mitchell, Robin Jarman, Roland Dumont, Paul Stickler, Colin Smith, Stuart Murray, Graham Nutcher and Martin Coleman for their constructive feedback. It was kind of them all to give so generously of their time. An especially big thank you to Sarah Ellis. I knew that English degree would come in handy sometime! Finally, my heartfelt thanks to John Hunt for his time, guidance, and expertise.

Contents

1.	First Night: Duty Calls	1
2.	Force(d) Entry	10
3.	Training School	16
4.	Local Procedure Course	42
5.	Parented Patrol	46
6.	Shirley Police Station	63
7.	Brewery Trip	71
8.	No Dignity in Dying	76
9.	Freedom of the City	83
10.	Shift Supervisory Encounters	92
11.	Hulse Road Police Hostel	98
12.	(Anti?) Social Adventures	112
13.	CID	124
14.	Area Beat Officers	130
15.	Accidents Don't Happen	136
16.	Football Duty	145

17.	Public Order Training	150
18.	(No) Angel Delight	154
19.	The End of the Beginning	162

Foreword

This account of my police probationary period from November 1980 to November 1982 includes applying and joining.

The transition from sixth former to police officer was full of new experiences, challenges, and, fortunately, humour. I feel privileged to have worked in a job that provided so many rich veins of incident in such a short period, and I am very grateful to all who played their part.

This irreverent "memoire" lets me share some of the entertaining and amusing events that occurred while documenting what policing was like (to my, at times, critical eye) in a period when the police were just beginning to see the need for reform after a demoralising and difficult 1970s.

This account is based on events that are true, to the best of my knowledge and belief (as it says on a witness statement form). The chronology has been affected by memory and the grouping of subjects. On one or two occasions, I borrowed from another time and fictionalised aspects of some vignettes very slightly and fairly obviously for added comic effect. Generally, I didn't need to. I have constructed fictitious characters with invented backstories to add to the enjoyment of the narrative and to respect the privacy of friends, colleagues, and the public.

Brian Mitchell
Hampshire
Autumn 2024

1 First Night: Duty Calls

You're like a long streak of piss!" the recruiting department constable observed as eloquently and sensitively as he was able. To be fair, I was standing on a scale that was not exactly overworked, given my weight was a comparatively light eleven and a half stone. Beside me was a measuring stick which was proving too short for the task of recording my height of six feet three. It was touch and go, which was leaner: the stick or me.

Self-conscious, due to a lack of clothing, except for my best underpants—trimmed in lurid lime green and from C&A—both fleetingly fashionable at the time, I faced a full-length upper floor window at Police Headquarters, Winchester. At least the lower pane was frosted, as my vital statistics were recorded by a weary but kindly looking force medical officer whose eyes were red as a Solent sunset. A rubber hammer tested my reflexes before I was instructed to drop my underpants. I complied before being asked by the FMO to bend over and cough. At this point, I was adjudged to have suffered enough humiliation and was declared fit. I was "in" with an official joining date, just a few weeks away, of November 12th, 1980. Welcome to Hampshire Constabulary.

A few weeks later, it's February 1981. It's dark. I was feeling chilly and apprehensive, like an exam was about to start. The inside of the white Ford transit van was stark: a phone handset, some radio buttons, and a fire extinguisher fixed to the floor. It was dirty but smelled of disinfectant, masking a faint odour of vomit: the kind that smells slightly acidic. The rear windows were barred, and a mesh grill separated the cab from the cell behind. My tunic was stiff and formal: I felt self-conscious. It wasn't warm, providing little insulation with the thin blue poly-cotton shirt beneath. I should have worn a pullover as a layer: schoolboy error.

Just a handful of minutes before finding myself shivering in the harshness of the van, I had been sitting on the edge of my seat in the functional "parade room" of Shirley police station, surrounded by an assorted bunch of policemen. Yes, all men. The lone woman police constable (WPC[1]) on the shift that night was "manning" the front enquiry office as her preferred duty to patrol. She doesn't

---

[1] WPC is a designation no longer in use.

like working nights or walking alone and says so. Some of the men don't like working nights or walking alone, but are less revealing.

The group looked rough in their dark, scruffy uniforms. The term uniform was only partially accurate as there were variations on display from tunics to pullovers, car coats, helmets, and hats, all in varying states of newness, smartness, and neglect. They reminded me of a troop of veteran infantry soldiers who had wearily made it through to 1945. The uniform was more Teutonic than Tommy. There was something almost industrial about this gathering. It was 9:45 p.m. on a Monday in February on a cold, seemingly quiet night in Southampton: an intimidating yet exciting place for a young man recently liberated from behind the school gates.

Abruptly, there was activity, and a group of us exited the station hurriedly. A "999" emergency call had been routed to the parade room phone: "Youth gone crazy with a knife". Two units are sent: Foxtrot Sierra 99 (the caged transit van or "pig" as it's known) and Panda[2] 7 (Ford Escort saloon), as the incident is in that vehicle's patrol area.

We pulled up on a damp council estate road outside a depressingly grey, concrete-rendered terraced house. White fluorescent light fell on the van's roof and illuminated the passenger side where I got out. A small group of "local youths" (police speak) were "loitering" (standing) by the street lamp and the gate to the house. I heard screaming and some sort of commotion inside. I was filled with exhilaration and expectancy and a sense that I needed to galvanise to do what's required in what might be a crucial early test.

"Just wait there, Brian," Instructed the driver, Stan, a large, imposing PC with a pronounced Gloucestershire County accent, leading to the nickname "Cruncher". Cruncher was wearing regulation shatterproof driving glasses with his cap sitting back on his porcine-like head. I had been allocated to his safekeeping for the night. He and Mark, the driver of Panda 7, went to the house. I was left standing in the street, like a spare biro refill —slender and black—but at the same time shiny, with gleaming buttons and helmet plate, trying to look official and dignified while unsure what I should be doing. The fluorescent light made me look newly minted, as if on display in a Marks and Spencer's shop window.

---

[2] Panda cars were originally two-tone blue and white medium-sized cars that did area beat work. They were still called pandas long after they were all white in colour.

The youths were obviously concerned for me. "Yeah, Brian," they mocked, "you just stay right there. Careful now."

And I had to. Flooded in light, clean, pressed, and barely older than them, I was all at sea beside a lifeboat shaped like a van. My "Burndept" personal radio was clipped to my lapel like in the TV show "Z Cars"; a position that looks good but isn't, as the device will fall at the first faint sign of movement. Fortunately, there was a harness designed to eliminate the possibility of damage.

Cruncher returned, and I was pointed to the house where a diminutive woman and an even smaller young girl were trembling at the foot of the stairs. I joined Mark on the first-floor landing. Mark was twenty-three but looked like he was delivered by forceps at forty: his head was indented at the temples, and his hair receded like a riptide at full moon.

The sixteen-year-old with the knife was locked in the toilet and wailing like a banshee, which was apt, as he was threatening to kill himself with the fervour of a sixteen-year-old who has consumed excessive quantities of the cider and lager mix known as "snakebite." (Such was its potency and ability to release the inner Tasmanian devil of your average wannabe Hells Angel, that one Bournemouth pub I knew had a stern warning on a notice outside: "Anyone asking for snakebite will be requested to leave the premises".) Our job was to assist this young man in leaving these premises while ensuring neither he nor we left the material world.

Mark's plan: he'll force the bathroom door with a screwdriver. My job: grab the Aussie marsupial/youth and pull him out without getting stabbed. By modern standards, this isn't a plan as it fails to consider the health and safety options: where's the negotiator, paramedics, public order shield team, and firearms backup? It was, however, *the* plan and a course of action that could lead to me having the shortest active service in policing history.

I prepared myself. I asked for this, dreamt about it, and watched it on TV. Now, I was living the dream. The wooden frame cracked and splintered as Mark forced open the door. A boy of about five feet six had smashed a mirror and smeared blood around the walls. He had a knife in his hand. I grabbed the glinting life-threatening arm and, with a speed suggesting I felt the quicker this was over, the better, I dragged him to the landing, where the three of us collapsed on the floor, with me holding his wrist with the determination of a pit bull embedded in a postman's posterior. The knife was released onto the thinly carpeted floor.

Remarkably, we were not issued handcuffs. Mark had his own, though: Hiatt 1960s. These were the Rolls-Royce of cuffs, I was later told, featuring a smooth swing through action: the preferred choice of serious law enforcement professionals and sadomasochists the world over. He passed them to me.

I forced the offending wrist into the cuff and clamped it shut. The second wrist got the same treatment, and the youth howled in agony. This remained the case all the way to Southampton Central police station. Later, I found that the handcuffs were oval-shaped, not round, and I forced the width of his wrist into the narrow part of the cuff, closing it against the bone. Although cuffs can be double-locked to stop them tightening, this was a bit redundant here—I was unaware of this feature, and anyway, they couldn't have closed any tighter. In fact, this was the first pair of handcuffs I'd ever seen in real life. They forgot that lesson at training school.

A bit later, Stan took me aside. "Mark says you did ok there, nipper."

I realised a test had been passed, all within the first hour of my first tour of duty. The slow handclap from the locals, as we put "the prisoner" in the back of the van, suggested they were less impressed with my and the constabularies' efforts, and this rather took the shine off any sense of self-satisfaction.

Around 1.40 a.m., we were summoned to a large, once-grand house on a broad avenue known as Hill Lane. Many of the surrounding houses were built for wealthy merchants, but as time passed, they became too expensive to keep up and often fell into the hands of landlords who converted them to bedsits. Occasionally, an elderly occupant would pass away, revealing gas lighting, servants' quarters, and large, high-ceilinged rooms with huge ornate fireplaces (often quickly scavenged by thieves). This was a grand Edwardian era, long gone. The room was dank and dark and smelled of stale socks, sweat, and spirits. The house itself, splendid in its structure, had been insecure and vacant and, consequently, an obvious shelter for the homeless.

Five men who had been sleeping rough were being questioned and "checked on PNC", meaning their details were run through the police national computer, a relatively recent innovation regarded as the great crime-fighting tool of its time.

The checking officer was Gareth Thruston, a large man wearing an open black Belstaff jacket with a cap bearing a waterproof cover pushed back atop his black, curly-haired head. He was coughing like a coalman in the damp and dust of the room and was clearly not well. Unsurprisingly, he went off sick later in the shift.

One man had a warrant outstanding for his arrest. As the new boy, I'd been called to do the actual arresting. My cap was pulled down in a serious-looking manner, making me resemble a guardsman. As I told the man, in my best formal "police speak", he was being arrested on a warrant he helpfully offered up, "I think there are three." Not according to the computer, there wasn't. However, a check of the manual warrants register showed he was spot on. Off we went to the city centre cell block again, tiled as it was in that shiny white porcelain brickwork so fashionable in the decorating of nineteen-thirties public toilets.

The rear of the civic centre police station was cobbled, and we rattled over the paving between two narrow rows of modest parked cars until we reached a large open doorway. This led to a covered area, open on the other side, creating a tunnel. Both doorways could be closed and were when prison vans with category "A" high-risk prisoners were being lodged at the station, pending the ferry to Parkhurst prison on the Isle of Wight.

I sat in the back of the van on a thin black PVC cushion running along the bench seats with the prisoner opposite, each of us holding the window grills for support. He was an amiable Midlander. Plucked from the obscurity of sleeping in an abandoned house, he seemed pleased to be the centre of attention and was, perhaps, relishing a heated cell and the welcome, if limited, refreshments to follow.

We assembled outside a massive steel door and pushed the button, notifying that we wanted entry. Eventually, the door swung open, and we were admitted by a sour-faced old sweat who clearly didn't relish more or, indeed, any work. We walked along the intimidating (to me, at any rate) corridor, past ancient cells. Outside some were pairs of shoes that indicated occupancy, like the red tab on the lock of a British Rail toilet. The cell block was called the Bridewell. It was part of the central police station, but also took longer-term prisoners from the two other stations to the west of the city: Shirley and Portswood. The sardonic, black-bearded custody sergeant told me the cells contained "the experiments". He was short, rotund, and tanned, and an image of a hairy cricket ball came to mind. I was told he was not the easiest of supervisors, and several PCs had wanted to hit him clear to the boundary.

The detained persons register was completed with the prisoner's help. Then there was the laborious listing of his personal property in long hand, his signing the record as correct, and the contents of his pockets; coins, scraps of paper, tobacco, and a bus ticket were all placed in a clear plastic bag and enclosed with a numbered seal, the digits being recorded on the log. An expired condom was included and seemed to sum up his prevailing luck.

Our prisoner was placed in a small, barred holding cell near the entrance door. The cell looked like a copy of one from the sheriff's office in a John Wayne movie. Stan and I then went and searched for the actual warrants in what was known as

The Bench Office. On our return, Mr Birmingham was cheerfully chatty; helpfully telling us he's committed a few burglaries extending from Bath to Bridport, and kindly gave a couple up locally to help boost the below-par detection figures. His confession earned him an unexpected mug of tea and a digestive biscuit.

Stan considered this crime wave a step too far for me on my first shift, so the lone night duty DC (detective constable) working across the west of the city was contacted and attended.

A young, slight detective named Norris Sharpe arrived and was brow beaten by Cruncher the arrest was about as much as I could be expected to manage and that CID should deal with. Norris couldn't easily resist Stan's train of thought, especially as the burglaries were alleged to have occurred on "central's patch", the DC's home station and, therefore, crucially, not ours to investigate. Game, set, and match to Cruncher, as Norris tentatively agreed to take them on. From this, I understood the rule: one police area doesn't usually investigate crimes committed in another.

In the van again, we clattered over the cobbles back to Shirley for tea and sandwiches and to "make up our pocket notebooks". Local legend has it that a constable, giving evidence at court, was asked, "When did you make up your notes, officer?"

Somewhat indignantly, the PC replied, "I never made them up; they're the truth!"

I spent the remainder of the shift as an observer in the Volvo area car with an easy-going PC called Nick "The Bishop" Church. Ironically, despite his name, in all the time I worked with him, I never saw him nick anyone. I established that Nick's "no fuss" approach to life meant he was a little shy. He got embarrassed driving the area car when it had lights flashing and two-tone horns blaring, so he often attended emergency calls with a minimalist approach: switching on the lights to pass through red traffic lights and then flicking them off immediately afterwards. I suppose the lack of sirens meant he nearly caught some burglars.

Nick told me a bit about himself and the area car concept. Now with twelve years of service, he had started his probation phase A in the New Forest. Until recently, the probationary period of two years had been split equally: Phase A and Phase B. Phase A was often a rural posting, and Phase B was city or urban. The idea was to give probationary constables, or "probbies" as they were known then (now called student officers), experience in different types of policing. Nick's phase B was Basingstoke, an urban area with a large rural expanse surrounding it. Officer numbers were low in the 1970s, partially due to appallingly low pay. Staff living in the south of Hampshire didn't usually want to be posted to the Northern Division, the beautiful expanse of territory from Winchester to Surrey and Berkshire, due to higher property prices. This translated to opportunities for PCs just out of probation. Nick had applied for an area car course and got it. The issue of inexperience was summed up by a detective who observed dryly, "It's all very well learning to drive a big car very fast, but you actually need to know what to do once you get there."

To Nick, the area car was seen as the plumb patrol position. No foot patrol work. A large plush Volvo 240 to swan around in. The car was supposed to be the first response to emergency 999 calls. The cars were double crewed initially, with two trained drivers who attended incidents, applied "first aid", and then left the paperwork to the minions on the shift. This was a model lifted from the aforementioned popular 1960s BBC TV show "Z Cars". For those "on area car", this was a dream come true: thrills and spills, high adrenaline with little paperwork afterwards. Over time, the concept became diluted with single crewing, the car becoming no more than a glorified "panda" (basic police vehicle). Still, area cars and transit vans had VHF radios, which meant the Force Control Room (FCR), situated at Headquarters, Winchester, could send 999 calls directly to them, something they couldn't do to panda vehicles, which were only contactable via the local station control room on the personal radio (PR) system.

I was to find that these VHF-equipped vehicles would spring into action without the rest of the station knowing about it. Many a time, the area car or van would fly past a walking PC, who would then radio into the station controller to find out what was going on. Even they wouldn't know until FCR contacted them via a system called "Mascot". This was akin to the ship's bridge calling down to the engine room: "FCR calling Foxtrot Sierra[3], Mascot". A voice would boom beside the local controller who sat in a glass-panelled booth in Shirley nick behind the front enquiry counter. Details of the call would then be passed by FCR for local resolution.

This was all new to me. Even then, I rather fancied the role. Who wouldn't? I did wonder, however, about my ability to pass the four-week driving course. Anyway, I could think about that later. My difficulty would be in trying to dispose of that probationer status in the next two years without them disposing of me.

---

[3] Foxtrot Sierra (FS) was the station designation for Shirley. The F for F Division, comprising the three stations in the west of the city, which included Portswood (FP) and Central (FC).

Nick relayed all of this, including repeating how tirelessly he and his crewmate had worked in their years at Basingstoke, as though this was a plausible excuse for substantially less activity in the remaining eighteen years of his service. As he spoke, I was "observing". This meant looking out the window while waiting for a call.

The car was equipped with a black telephone handset (like the van) and a VHF radio, which could be programmed by a dual dial to update a unit's "state", which was then notified to the force control room. State 94 meant "meal break" and was, predictably, the most used. "State 95" meant arrived and dealing. State 01 meant single crewed; 02 double crewed. The idea was good, but not much used in practice: it was quicker to update states verbally using the handset.

State codes were printed on a personal issue card and were designed to prevent eavesdroppers from understanding what the police were dealing with or how often they went for a cup of tea. These state codes became part of the policing language of the time. Officers would say to colleagues in the corridor, "I'm going 94". The codes were even extended to off-duty activities. If communicating they were going to a party, one officer might enquire of another, "You going 01 (singly) or 02 (double crewed, i.e., with a partner)?" Of course, this kind of arcane language wasn't just the preserve of the police; the military has its own jargon and considerably more acronyms.

There was an emergency button on the radio control panel, which rendered the vehicle's radio mic live. On the few occasions it was activated, by a negligent knee perhaps or a knicker removing knuckle (usually during the quieter part of a night), the control room would enquire saucily, "Who's pressed the bonk button?" Unsurprisingly, this muted the heavy breathing somewhat, and the unscheduled radio show would come to an abruptly unhappy ending.

From the driver's left, the area car had a row of buttons. These controlled the blue light, sirens, and illuminated signs. Then there was the radio. One officer told me that when he'd got in the area car for the first time, the somewhat self-important driver had said to him, "All these buttons are *mine*. That (pointing to the radio) is *yours*." The probationer was unimpressed, and his descriptor of the driver was short, precise, and consisted of in letters exactly the number of buttons the driver had exclusive control over: four.

We drove along Windermere Avenue, on Millbrook Estate. All was deathly quiet. They say you are closer to being dead at 4 a.m. than at any other time while asleep. I can believe it. Two young men in their teens ducked down behind a parked car beside the footpath. We stopped, and they popped up, like expired parking meters going into a penalty charge. Nick "stop checked" the two of them. There was no power of search, but he invited them to turn out their pockets. They had nothing on them and little to say. I recorded their details on small pink stop check forms that I submitted to the "collator" (later known as the field intelligence officer). These were my first-ever "stops."

I didn't know it then, of course, but both would develop into fully fledged criminals. One would get his nose broken in a fight with police, leading to a PC being charged with GBH, then acquitted at the neutral venue of Bournemouth Crown Court, thirty-five miles to our west. The other would become a walk-in thief, known throughout the city for his sticky fingers, until a premature death in a foreign capital from a drug overdose cured his kleptomania.

We returned to the station at 5:25 a.m. and completed paperwork. I was given a box file with my name on it and a slot to put it in alongside the names of the rest of my shift, which numbered around sixteen officers. Radios were placed in the radio room, with batteries inserted in chargers and replaced with full ones. Promptly at 5:45 a.m., we exited into the station yard. The early shift was already about. Some detectives had appeared to make some early morning arrests. It wasn't unusual, but equally, the patrol officers regarded it as a novelty. One PC commented on the CID's early presence,

"Why are you lot in? Shit the bed?"

I drove my sensible green Renault 12, bought with eight hundred pounds saved diligently these last few weeks. It had sat immobile for six months, its previous owner having expired along with the road tax. This might be the reason why, at 5:54 precisely, it chose to break down at Oakley Road traffic lights, to my utter horror, spluttering into inactivity like a drowning drake.

I pushed it partly off the road, at what would be a busy junction later, and jogged to my digs in a state of high concern. I knew no one here. I was skint. After climbing into the dark wood-framed bed, I was up again at 9:30 to run to a phone box outside a pub, well named "The Fighting Cocks", to call my dad and a close school chum for help. They were thirty miles away. It was going to be a long day and a longer night. No mobile phones or complimentary AA cover on your insurance in 1981. No Green Flag. No "I want to be a Millionaire," just, fortunately, family and friends.

2 Force(d) Entry

As Nick "The Bishop" had outlined,1970s police pay had been pretty dire, with some police families qualifying for supplementary benefit, a social security payment made when income levels were too low. This affected recruiting numbers and quality.

The Labour government initiated a pay review under Lord Edmund Davis. Reporting in the late seventies, it recommended substantial pay increases. The government accepted the expensive recommendations but decided to split implementation over twelve months, with half being paid in September 1978 and the other half a year later in September 1979.

Margaret Thatcher was an ardent supporter of law and order and, at the time, an ardent supporter of the police. She stated that her government would implement the pay deal immediately if elected. It came to pass, with a considerable number of police votes, that the conservatives were elected in May 1979, and they proceeded to do just that. It took time to implement, but officers did get the September pay rise a few weeks early. This was a spectacular PR win for the Tories, as many police officers associated the pay rise with the Conservatives and completely forgot that the Labour government had done all the legwork. Indeed, so rapturous was the regard by many for Thatcher that, when I tried to calmly explain the reality of the pay deal to one of my slightly more right-leaning colleagues, "Sinn Féin" Shaughnessy, he animatedly waved a partially jam-covered knife under my nose in a fit of apoplectic denial that was, arguably, a recordable assault. Like the lady, he was not for turning.

Good times had dawned; police pay was changing. As a consequence, by the time I was applying for the position of constable, forces were filling up, and the competition became fierce. I'd really had my mind set on policing since the age of four. Prior to that, I confess to a degree of ambivalence. I had read Critchley's "A History of Police in England and Wales" and saw the statistic that only ten per cent of officers had "O" levels, and just one per cent had an "A" level or more. Whatever the exact numbers, they weren't impressive. Graduates were like gold dust, numbering just a few hundred in the entire service. I had been confident of getting in the top ten per cent by banking a few "O" levels, including the necessary English and maths, so I didn't particularly feel a need to keep my pedal to the metal.

Along with an aspirant officer school friend, Sally (who later opted to conduct investigations as a radiographer), we drove in her ageing mini to The Metropolitan Police Training School at Hendon on a cold, thickly fog-bound day in November 1979 to attend an afternoon recruitment event. The traffic was as heavy as the fog, and crossing the North Circular was a feat as heroic as I've ever witnessed, given that, as we traversed, it was impossible to see what was coming. Dirty grey lorries loomed large out of the gloom like rogue elephants, and we were relieved to get across the incessant flow of impatient traffic. Eventually, the little car limped into the dank, mist-shrouded car park in North West London. For two teenagers from the sticks, this was an adventure into the great, scary unknown.

Shortly, we found our way to the warmth of a low-lit, cavernous lecture theatre, like I'd seen in the movie "Doctor in the House". Instead of a medical school dean, though, there stood a cheery, hyper-confident training sergeant by the name of Savage.

Born a cockney, it seemed, given his accent, he had a smile broader than the Thames, but with it, a hard, no-nonsense glint in eyes framed with a Teutonic jawline and shock of blonde hair. Sergeant Savage had an air of invincibility, as though there was nothing within the confines of the jurisdiction of the Greater London Council he couldn't deal with.

He greeted the assembled group, which numbered around forty. A few questions followed. A well-nourished chap, with thick black spectacles and prematurely thinning hair, was wrapped in a heavy woollen overcoat and sat down the front like a school swot. Coiled around his neck was an overly long green and yellow university scarf that looked like a soporific python. He immediately asked about academic qualifications, presumably on the grounds that, unlike most of the potential recruits in the theatre, he actually possessed some.

"Policing is more than academic qualifications, my old son," came the put-down the rest of the hall wanted to hear.

After the short introductory session, we were shown a film about life in "The Met"[4]. Apologies were made that the film was from the late 1960s. It depicted a young constable getting into scrapes and japes and was mostly amusingly light-hearted, but serious where needed. It was quite an uplifting account of working in London in the swinging sixties, expressing energy, excitement, and camaraderie that filled the theatre with a good positive vibe.

---

[4] https://www.huntleyarchives.com/preview.asp?image=1085159

Not for long. At the conclusion of the movie, Savage, standing completely still and deadly, deadly serious, announced, "That young PC was stabbed to death on Clapham Common shortly after that film was made. Don't think this job's a breeze. Enjoy your trip home."

The event was over. The mood in the theatre had changed from optimism to depression. It was like leaving a cinema after watching the movie "Apocalypse Now": total shocked silence. The audience shuffled out into the murky, unwelcoming darkness, feeling mixed up and uncomfortable. How bizarre. What were the chances that the central character of a recruiting film would be killed, given there were thousands of Met officers and so few fatalities? Years later, I was to find fragments of that film on something unknown to us at that time: the internet. It also helped me identify that young PC, whose smiling, fun-filled face is indelibly imprinted on my mind: PC Michael John Davies, aged 23, who was stabbed off duty in the back after warning a man harassing his wife and friends on 19th August 1969. RIP John.

Despite the gloomy ending to the recruiting event, the capital seemed the place to be, given the career opportunities and the ability to lose oneself in both work and fog. However, a letter from London telling me I'd have to defer my application for two years due to a recurrent childhood illness sent me into a paroxysm of activity. There were forty-three forces, and like a prisoner on death row pleading for clemency, I was prepared to write to them all. Fortunately, that wasn't necessary.

I applied to Hampshire Police again after they sent me the wrong application forms: I hadn't wanted to be a traffic warden in Waterlooville. I completed their rather appealingly pale blue sheets that seemed inspired by Basildon Bond writing paper. The recruiting sergeant described the force as being liberally minded, whatever that meant. Whatever it did mean, he was right: I was offered an interview and medical. Like a wallaby on speed, I literally jumped for joy at the news.

The first hurdle, though, was an interview by my home force, Dorset, followed by a home visit, presumably to ensure there were no prostitutes on the premises, crumbs on the carpet, or anything beyond medicinal brandy and a bible in the drinks cabinet. I was issued a travel warrant dated 26th March 1980 and embarked on a circuitous journey to their force headquarters, an office block at the Atomic Energy Establishment at Winfrith.

I arrived by bus, train, and finally, shuttle bus. There, I sat with several other nervous hopefuls. These included a soldier whose dress sense was a suit matched perfectly with a shirt unbuttoned to the midriff. On display was a yellow metal medallion, presumably on loan from J. Arthur Rank or purloined from the foyer of a Chinese restaurant. In tasteful contrast, there was a background redolent of a dark shag pile rug. I don't know how he got on, but it did appear to amount to a sartorial slip-up as I overheard one of the assessors observing to a colleague,

"Is he here for a job as a policeman or a pimp?"

I like to think he pulled a trick and turned it around in his interview. The format of the morning, according to my letter, was the police entrance exam for two hours, then an interview. As I had the necessary four "O" levels in my back pocket, I was somewhat bemused by this. It proved to be a pro forma letter.

"Mr Mitchell?"

I put my hand up as though I was about to ask to go to the toilet.

"You're not having the exam, so it's interview for you now."

Seconds later, I was plonked in front of an avuncular chief inspector who amiably asked a few questions about my family background (professional), where I lived (quite acceptable), and my motivation to join (exceptional[5]). It was all over in ten minutes, and before I knew it, I was back on the minibus heading from the train station and its once-every-four-hour service, dedicated in the main, I surmised, to the moving of sheep and nuclear waste.

The home visit never materialised. I assume I conveyed such a cosy perception of broad middle-class banality that the inspector decided not to bother getting some poor sergeant to drive out for an inspection. My house-proud mother was bitterly disappointed. It's interesting that the police did these visits. What standards of social acceptability were applied? How did it affect who joined? Who did it exclude? I wondered how the sergeant got on at Medallion Man's brothel.

Eventually, after months of waiting, the big interview day in Hampshire was upon me. I was edgy with anticipation. The imposing tower block of Police Headquarters made the experience particularly tense. Of course, I was concerned about the medical, although, in truth, there wasn't anything to fear. I simply had to get that far, cough, and hope my testicles moved the requisite distance. It was interview first before lunch.

There were nine of us, four ex-servicemen, one ex-employee of Ladbrokes, a rangy electrician (for balance, all middling to ugly), a pretty, petite, clever sixth former (they say girls grow up quicker: this one was living with a boyfriend of

---

[5] With a charismatic uncle in the job, I blame it mainly on him and a TV diet of "Z Cars" and "Dixon of Dock Green". The combination of personality, uniform, projected power and beneficence, reflected back through the moralistic lens of television, was captivating.

thirty and as a consequence terrified me) and a red-haired young woman who was well scrubbed and presented but dressed slightly shabbier than the rest of us in a powder blue skirt and top. I sensed she was from a rougher background. We talked politely, if anxiously. Miss Powder Blue was called Joanne and came from Slough. It had been her life's ambition to join the police, she told me excitedly. A couple of her brothers were known to the police for minor matters, but clearly, that wasn't the path for her.

Small talk over, I found myself being interviewed by the assistant chief constable responsible for personnel and training. A former London officer, he was middle-aged, slightly overweight and with the kind of build that did not make him either impressive or imposing, which helped calm my nerves. These moments can be life-defining. He displayed a warm humanity and asked questions I could answer fairly easily, particularly regarding my motivation.

The crippler question was, "How can a young man of nineteen deal with a domestic dispute?"

I argued logically: there was no reason I couldn't do it if others at the same age had managed. It was the best I could come up with, but I felt my response hadn't quite convinced him, as to be honest, it hadn't convinced me. We got to the end of his questions, or maybe the half hour was up.

"Ok, Mr Mitchell," he sighed. "You can have your medical. By the way, the answer to the domestic disputes question is, we will train you."

And that was it. I was almost in! And yet, because I didn't fully believe it, I couldn't let myself experience the relief. None of the others had been told they had passed their interviews. We had been informed that we would be told after lunch. So, it was only me who had been told in advance, and I didn't want to share my news in case I had misheard. I was left with an out-of-body feeling. I was through, wasn't I? At least I could try and enjoy some of the headquarters' food, which had a school dinner feel to it, with steamed pudding and custard on the menu. We were spared eating with our inquisitors, as they were in the senior officers' mess. While they were being served fish, chips and peas by waitresses in black and white uniforms, we lined up on the other side of the kitchen at the hatch in the blue-collar section, not unlike the inmates of the prison just over the wall from us.

I later established that the rule of the senior officers' dining room was that entry was permitted to chief inspectors and above. Inspectors (senior officers, but seemingly not senior enough) could enter if accompanied by an adult, sorry, officer senior to themselves. Thus, ambitious inspectors would "casually" enquire of their bosses whether they were peckish in the hope of being spirited past security into a world of silver service and getting their faces noticed by the hierarchy in preparation for promotion boards. Imagine the anxiety for some aspirational inspector, having to make polite small talk with the chief constable while balancing bullet-like peas on a fork.

After lunch, I noticed Joanne being spoken to softly by two of the recruiting staff. She looked distressed and, at one point, blushed before bursting into tears as she was led away, as though she didn't want to go. After we had all been formally notified of our success, the recruiting sergeant divulged that Joanne came from a family of seven children. Quite what this had to do with anything, I have no idea. Maybe she just got the wrong interviewer or had a bad day. No one spoke, but there was a collective sense of disquiet among those left. Maybe somebody had to fail?

It's a truism that life goes on, and, as we all still had the medical to pass, Joanne was quickly forgotten. We were to become police officers, assuming we passed this next assessment. So it was that I found myself that afternoon standing beside a part-frosted window on the fifth floor of police headquarters in my underpants, being measured and weighed like a prize fighter without the build to match and being described by a grizzled old PC as resembling a spurt of urine. Nice. I bent over and "coughed," had my reflexes checked and had the satisfaction of kicking the doctor, who should have known better than to sit so close and at that angle.

After the doctor's recovery, the examination was indeed a formality in its simplicity. He seemed like a latter-day Noah, checking I had pretty much two of everything. I dryly reflected on all the effort and applications that had gone before. If this one force hadn't been flexible, I wouldn't be here now, but then again, if my legs had been shorter, I might be flying an attack aircraft. Not true, though. With my mathematical ability, I'd have cocked up the coordinates and bombed Basingstoke. It's a funny world. The only reason I hadn't applied to Hampshire earlier was that they sent me the wrong forms. I could barely believe it. I'd gone from sixth form via blue form to uniform. I had a job!

3 Training School

My start day was a Wednesday in November. Three days of induction at Police HQ followed. I'd been instructed to have a haircut in advance. I shouldn't have bothered. The cut was judged as insufficiently severe for training school, and so I, with a couple of others, were sent off to a local "barber". Barbarous is how I'd describe the assault that followed. I presumed the hairdresser was an Australian, with a background in sheep farming, given the quantity of hair piled up around my chair. At least he refrained from holding me by my ankles. Outside the shop, my ears were noticeably colder in the autumnal air. The "short back and sides" was not a style ragingly popular since the nineteen fifties and about as trendy as Jacob Rees-Mogg at a Sex Pistols concert. Essentially still a schoolboy, I was being made to feel like one.

I found the police and fashion had been an uncomfortable pairing. When flared trousers were all the rage in the early seventies, the police had apparently petitioned for slightly trendier trousers than the straight-legged uniform issue. After grumbling and rumbling, the slowly whirling wheels of the Home Office bureaucracy reluctantly turned out a slightly flared design, just in time for the fashion to die, making the service look like it was entrenched in 1973. A change of headgear and your average copper could have been confused with Noddy Holder.

Having been instructed to bring a suitcase, we headed to uniform stores to be kitted out before travelling to the regional training school at Ashford in Kent on the following Sunday.

Tailoring might have been offered at Hepworths or Dorothy Perkins, but it certainly wasn't offered at the outfitters of any of Her Majesty's Constabularies to the lower ranks. Here you got your size or the nearest approximation.

There were forty-three police forces in England and Wales. You might suppose it would have made financial sense for them all to have the same uniform to benefit from bulk buying. Well, think again. Forty-three forces meant forty-three different uniforms. There were very close similarities, of course, and shared suppliers, but each force had its own sartorial style, as was very evident at the regional training school, where uniform envy was rife.

Occupying the bottom position in the cool cop's couture awards was the British Transport Police, almost exclusively due to their nylon shirts. I can only assume the person who negotiated that contract was someone who wasn't going to wear them in the heat of a searing summer on the tube. Perhaps they got a good deal from a brand in Brentford. The good news for BTP officers was that they didn't need to iron their shirts. The bad news was that they did need to wash them very regularly. BTP officers were often to be seen scratching like they had suffered a force-wide outbreak of scabies. In reality, it was just heat rash—in November.

At the top end of the envy echelon were the gals and guys from "the city". This small force of just under a thousand officers policed the square mile containing the capital's financial district and had the Corporation of the City of London bankrolling them, and it showed. Their uniforms were made of a luxurious, shimmering blue material with fetching golden adornments. Much photographed by tourists and often ceremonially deployed, the final decadent flourish was each officer's collar number individually inscribed on their helmet plate. No such embellishments for us new recruits on the South Coast. My number was written on the lining of my helmet in black biro from a Bic pen.

In Hampshire, there was a clear demarcation between officers joining pre-May 1979 and those who joined just post-budget cuts, courtesy of the new government's strategy of austerity. Before, equipment was lavish. There were capes (ideal for keeping chips hidden and warm) and very heavy but incredibly smart greatcoats, resembling those from the cavalry charge in Dr Zhivago. (You couldn't have mounted a horse wearing one, and if you fell in deep water, you'd drop like a depth-charged dredger.) Post-plebiscite, and the cosy capes and glorious greatcoats had gone.

Instead, recruits were issued with a raincoat made of a rubberised material called "Gannex". It was mildly rainproof but had no thermal lining. Provided in conjunction as a cost-effective winter coat substitute (according to someone who sat in a warm office in the procurement department), it was a feebly thin, sleeveless body warmer made of lightly quilted nylon. The combination was woeful and very ineffective against the cold. Furthermore, the shoulders of the coats weren't fitted but, through some ancient, presumably Elizabethan cost-saving construction, ballooned outwards inelegantly as though inflated. Adding to the look of the not-so-dapper PC about town was a Custodian helmet, which, if slightly oversized, rendered the wearer visionless, as though crowned with a black bucket. One ex-navy colleague had such an outsized helmet that he was christened "shed head". There was enough room in it to build a battleship.

The Custodian was a reinforced helmet designed to protect the wearer from a heavy blow, unlike the older and much-prized style, which was constructed of a mixture of a kind of paper-mâché and felt. The real benefit of this older design of helmet was not apparent to me until the day a veteran beat cop, "Thumper" Owen, who possessed a face like a butcher's block, removed his and promptly folded it flat and then again into a quarter, helmet plate included. At this point, his eyes twinkling and grinning broadly, he surreptitiously slipped it into his trouser pocket.

"And that nipper, is what you does when you go's for a beer," he confided conspiratorially, in an accent that at the time would have ruled him out as a BBC announcer but today would probably guarantee employment.

Apparently, going for a beer was something he did do. One day he was found slumbering in a hedgerow adjacent to his favourite refreshment spot, helmet firmly planted in his pocket like a dark blue and chrome pasty.

So, I was duly issued with a helmet, cap with waterproof cover, tunics and trousers, a belt, shirts, clip-on tie (to prevent strangulation) and my coat with liner and two sweaters.

Of the pullovers, one was a thin V-necked, very navy-blue woollen jumper that was a godsend for warmth, while the other was a NATO-style combat sweater with shoulder and elbow patches. This latter item was unique nationally: only Hampshire had this deviation from the policing uniform norm, and so, of course, we were banned from wearing them at training school as they were seen as overly avant-garde. The fact that these NATO sweaters were comfortable, cheaper than tunics, worn by the military, whose uniform our uniform was based on, did not sway the conservative rump of the service's fashion police. Hampshire sweaters were a threat to the natural order of civilised society and could not be tolerated. If they were accepted, it would only lead to a spiral of decline into the acceptance of comfortable clothing, body armour, stubble, tattoos and charity bands.

I was also issued with a rosewood truncheon, a rubberised torch and leather gloves. A Hampshire crested pocket notebook cover was provided, along with various inserts covering assorted topics from incident codes, unexploded bomb procedures and how to deliver a baby. I felt Royal Mail might be the safest option regarding delivery after a maternity unit. I was definitely in third place, given my inability to hold on to a bar of soap or competently deal with linguini. There is, by the way, no truth in the urban myth that a pregnant woman has the lawful right to urinate in a police officer's helmet. Indeed, why would she need to, given the kerb side is perfectly adequate on most weekends for so many of her nocturnal sisters and, indeed, brothers?

Away from the delights of uniform stores, an important event to be completed was attestation. This is where Constables are sworn in by a local JP. To add to the sense of occasion, the event was thoughtfully held in the gym, which doubled as a store and had no natural light. A few jumbled manila boxes bore silent and solemn witness. We dutifully agreed to serve our sovereign lady, the queen, as we held a bible aloft with one hand and read from a card in the other. We faced the magistrate, who was elevated behind a small lectern adjacent to a vaulting horse, over which was draped a sweaty piece of discarded underwear beside what appeared to be a jockstrap. It took slightly longer than saying grace, but it had the same outcome as we ate immediately afterwards. Over lunch, we were commended by the training staff. The JP had mentioned how impressed she was at our reciting the oath without any mistakes. Essentially, she was impressed that we were able to read and speak at the same time. I concluded I could expect to be patronised similarly in the months to come. I wondered if training school might have lessons on basic skills for a county constable: forelock-tugging and advanced police pencil licking, perhaps?

After lunch, we were encouraged to line up in height order in our brand new and unfamiliar uniforms. We were then given an "inspection" as a precursor to what was to come at Ashford. Footwear, which we supplied ourselves, was examined, and the ex-bookmaker, possibly hedging his bets in case he failed the course, had elected to wear a pair of black brogues with an attractive pattern on the toe cap. This anomaly was pointed out by the recruiting officer, who issued an instruction to find something with a plain toe cap as opposed to "a bloody doily". I took the footwear challenge seriously and had a large pair of inflexible Doctor Martens boots. These felt like they had been previously owned by a deep-sea diver and chaffed my heels like they contained a cheese grater.

On the completion of these three days of admin, we lugged our overflowing suitcases to our respective homes, aware we would be travelling back on Sunday to get to the district training centre by mid-afternoon for further induction. Over the weekend, I assembled the list of items needed. Apparently, a sports jacket was required for the bar. I was only planning on going for a quiet drink, not attending a wedding.

After a two-hour trip in Alex the electrician's Ford Cortina, we arrived at what was a sanatorium in a past life, as far as I could see, and which was then a centre of regional policing educational excellence. That's what it said on the flyer they gave me, anyway. I was going to be here for ten weeks: five on either side of Christmas, with a two-week break in the middle. Bonus.

On the drive down, I mused over what training school would be like. Given a constable's extensive range of authority, I thought the curriculum would be professionally focused, majoring in law, along with social awareness training on how to police a mixed society (the term diversity didn't exist then). I expected the course to be reasonably open-minded, given the complex environment the police occupied, and I expected to be treated like an adult. I was in for a rude awakening, with perhaps one exception on a Wednesday afternoon.

At the reception, we checked in with colleagues from across the South East and were allocated our nameplates, room and class details. We were then sent off to find our male-only residential block. If you were found in the female block, you would be thrown off the course *in disgrace*. Rather intriguingly, no mention was made of what happened to women found in male quarters. Presumably, a woman found wandering in a male block would be deemed lost rather than a pervert and potential sex pest. Alex and I were on different floors. I located my four-man room and dumped my gear on the only bed that was left.

We had to be in the main hall at four for our "welcome" by the deputy commandant. Having arrived early, we sat expectantly, like nervous children on their first day at school. The room was filled with what seemed like around a hundred people, but no one spoke. The atmosphere was uncomfortable. Surrounding us, like stewards at an event, stood the training sergeants. One, from Sussex, immaculately resplendent in broad silver stripes and a slashed peak cap, marched up and down the aisles, occasionally throwing out a morsel of advice.

"Watch out for the horse and rabbit pie. It's made of equal proportions of horse and rabbit—one horse to one rabbit."

We sniggered quietly, waiting for the chief inspector.

The main doors to the hall banged open. I glanced over the shoulder of my jacket, which was the texture of a cheap sack. I saw an unhappy-looking sandy-haired man in uniform. He had a sheaf of papers tucked under his left arm that subtly bolstered his self-importance.

He stood at the lectern. This was no greeting or welcome, just a red-faced rant of such ferocity I feared for his cardiac health. I was somewhat stunned. He hoped we would fail. Discipline would be tough. Break the rules, and you get thrown out. Then, in a hurricane of hypertension and half-dropping papers he never referred to, he stalked out, leaving behind a room full of perturbed probationers. I was transported to the warden's speech in the movie Papillon when the prisoners arrived at the French penal colony. The only significant difference I could see was the warden there was friendlier. To balance things, though, at least we weren't threatened with a guillotine. I did wonder if the chief inspector might previously have been a detective, given his hardman act. Of course, his near pantomime performance was a conspiracy, as immediately afterwards, the sergeants moved in to do the good cop routine, bringing us under their protective wings, where we, with some relief, compliantly formed into our classes to do introductions.

This was to be home for two and a half months. There was an intake every five weeks of around 60 to 70 student officers, split into four classes. In the main, they came from forces located in the South East. I was a member of "A" class. There were two training sergeants per class whose job it was to mould us (or beat the resistant, like sheet metal) into police officers and get us through the 10 weeks and back to pavement pounding in our home provinces.

Each instructor was on a two-year Home Office-funded secondment with accommodation provided on-site. Most were married but arrived single, with several choosing to live that lifestyle Monday to Friday. The reasons for being in training and out of force were usually a desire for promotion or a desire to be away from home. In short: desire. One hulking rugby-playing instructor, Matt Truss, was reputed to have shrunken to a shadow of his former self as a result of the physical endeavours of running up the several flights of steps between his ground-floor quarters and those of a rather stunning colleague who was resident on the all-female top tier. She, on the other hand, displayed a healthy radiance, which was, no doubt, appreciated by her husband when she arrived home on a Friday night, full of the joys of spring. (Even in November.)

Our sergeants were Dan Sower, a small man with a dark, acrid sense of humour who hailed from Hertfordshire and his less intense sidekick from Suffolk, Bob "The Bell Ringer" Pew: so named on account of his being an internationally competitive campanologist. They chimed well together, with Dan full of urban urgency and Bob more bucolically focused, with a particularly comprehensive knowledge of The Animals Act of 1911. He also had a comprehensive knowledge of the Sexual Offences Act. The ease with which he was able to integrate the two into various examples proved mildly disconcerting.

In class, we were each required to "think on our feet". This meant getting up every time we spoke. Each student had a chair that sat on a curved metal bar, allowing it to slide back effortlessly. All except me. My chair had a traditional configuration of four legs, making pushing back against the carpet tiles more of a struggle than I'd have liked. This suggested to the instructors I was less enthusiastic than was the case as I tried to haul myself upright, often almost semi-disembowelling myself on the table's edge.

I sat quietly, perspiring in the warmth of the classroom, with the fear of public speaking making my heart pump. Aware that just a few rudimentary sentences might be beyond some recruits (me at this juncture), our lines were prompted by headings on the whiteboard: who are you, and where are you from? I was surprised they didn't immediately start with date and place of birth, followed by address and "Where do you think you are going at this time of night?" However, this would have been too much all at once. I managed to provide the required personal information and noted down the names of my classmates. We then shuffled off to dinner, where the budget of a pound a day for all meals per student had left a significant underspend. Still, there were crisps available to be purchased later in the bar to make up for any vitamin deficiencies from the dining hall fare.

Before a drink, I went to our accommodation with three of my classmates and now roommates for the next two and a half months. Having bagged the best bed in the room, it was no surprise that Dave Roach was an ex-squaddie trading one uniform for another. Serious but also funny, he possessed a huge dark macho moustache. He was voted class leader for drill purposes the next day and got to wear a blue lanyard. He was so proud of this that we contemplated stitching it to his pyjamas.

Cleve Forrester was a nineteen-year-old from a seaside town. He had the build of Charlton Heston and the sexual energy of a rhesus monkey. A gifted and active athlete, he had an insomniac girlfriend with whom he spent his weekends. Cleve needed all the shut-eye he could get in the week and achieved this by sleeping in class, getting up at the last moment and walking around in a haze of soporific confusion, which regularly got him in difficulty. By week six, he was yet again reporting for a late evening parade for a breach of discipline. He was confronted by the duty inspector.

"In the shit again, Forrester?" enquired the duty officer. Stoically, Cleve replied.

"I'm always in the shit, sir. It's just the depth that varies."

Peter "Taffy" (nicknames were nothing but inventive in the police) Pool was a conscientious, compassionate man who had changed career from junior supermarket manager in Merthyr to search for the meaning of life. Despite pontificating over this subject many times in the bar, we never found it. Peter was a man constantly battling with his weight. Given the quality of the first night's dinner, he may just have found the regime he was after: the look and leave-it diet.

So, it was with these three amigos that I had the pleasure of sharing a room. As you do when you live with people, you discover things, little personal things, like the fact that each of them had won a regional snoring competition.

Each morning, there was a parade. This involved marching in full uniform and then an inspection. On the first morning, the commandant, an elegantly tall, slim man with an aquiline nose and the bearing of a Caesar, tersely informed me that my boots were insufficiently gleaming or, to use the military term, bulled, meaning there was not a mirror-like shine on the toe cap. Quite why there should be was rather beyond me: I hadn't joined The Grenadiers Guards, and I had a mirror for shaving. To be fair to factual accuracy, he had a point; there was only a dull glow on my boots, creating an outline of a face if one peered close and hard enough. It was like looking at a person through a misted bathroom window (a pastime of some bored patrolling PCs I was to later establish). I was disappointed: I'd been spitting like a camel and polishing like a puritan for ages. My efforts, though, had all been in vain.

Following up behind the commandant was the drill sergeant, a small and unusually benevolent former soldier called Sergeant Bond. His job was to get us to march properly and try to instil and maintain a military-like level of smartness.

"What kind of polish you using, son?" he asked gently, looking up at me from under a slashed peak, swagger stick tucked under his arm and pointed towards my chest.

"Tuxan Sarge."

"That'll be your problem then. Get yourself some Kiwi that'll sort you out."

As the expert in all matters relating to boot maintenance, he was absolutely right. Kiwi applied with a little water and a soft cloth with the tip of one's finger for approximately 20 minutes would eventually produce a mirror-like shine that you would then spend the rest of the day trying to protect from being scraped off. This was a difficult objective to achieve and certainly would not survive enemy action: on return to force, a rather vile and juvenile PC, with shoes as dull as he was, deliberately dragged his boot across my toe caps in an act that was only slightly short of criminal damage. Some people just don't like being outshone. Actually, we used saliva: "spit and polish", as it was called. This was phased out in favour of water by the Health and Safety brigade, spurred on, in all probability, by the Department for the Control of Infectious Diseases.

Continuing with the follow-up inspection and gazing down at my Dr Martens footwear, Bond also observed wryly, "While you're at it, lad, you might like to re-lace those boots. They look like an old lady's corset."

I hadn't considered there might be a masculine way of lacing boots, but I did have to agree that the crossover lattice effect I had achieved was more appropriate on a cherry tart. Or, as was later noted by one of my roommates, a tart called Cherry.

A recruit's big concern at the morning parade was the inspecting officer noticing something wrong that would lead to them handing out corrective punishment, which was referred to as "a nine o'clock parade". This meant parading in full uniform at nine p.m. in front of the duty sergeant rather than parading in front of the bar staff smelling of cheap aftershave.

These should have been sparingly handed out to the shoddy, dishevelled individuals who had never been properly introduced to irons (BTP excluded, of course) or shaving with a mirror. They were, though, handed out like condoms at a family planning clinic in the first weeks, presumably as a very rough tool in the pursuit of uniformed perfection, but more likely just to make the going tough. Any minor infraction could attract this sanction. Of particular interest to the inspecting officers in the first days were welts. Instructors would peer into the seams of boots, where leather met sole, searching for polish. Failure to polish in the welts and on the sides of the soles led to a nine o'clock appointment with the duty officer. This changed quite quickly in the next few days after the head of housekeeping objected to the amount of polish that was proving impossibly stubborn to remove from the carpets. Instruction reversed. Do not polish your welts. (And bad luck to those censured before this instruction.)

I only found myself subjected to a nine o'clock parade once: a minor crease was noticed in the blue Dymo embossed tape on my name badge as a result of it falling off and having to be stuck back on. The question I wanted answering, but didn't feel brave enough to ask, was, were we expected to treat the public in such an arbitrary, petty fashion when eventually released upon them? I'm pretty sure the answer would have been no. There was no discretion for students, and yet we were expected to apply it in our dealings with the public. We were, of course, being trained to a military model that required more obedience than independent thought. I learned later that a review of training led to significant changes from 1985 onwards. Five years too late for me.

It was day two, and I was not yet into the routine of Ashford life. I had the worst bed in our quarters: against the wall on the other side of which lay a much-used lavatory, apparently housed in an amplification chamber. My bed was the only one of the four with an adjacent locker that had a padlock rather than a lock with a code. System failure imminent.

On the Tuesday morning, I found I'd padlocked my key in the locker. Epic panic followed. All my clothes were inside, except boots and helmet. Frantically, I assembled a uniform which was a collage of colleagues' clothing along the corridor. They found the sight of me scuttling about in my shorts, like a traumatised tramp begging for clothing, decidedly amusing. On parade, the focus was on welts, not lapels, so the foreign badges of Essex Police that did not match my helmet plate were missed. I was forced to eat stylistic humble pie, though, and to be truly grateful to the BTP for the loan of a nylon shirt. I scratched like a Scottish wildcat and endured a succession of minor static electric shocks, but, nevertheless, I was very appreciative. Washing and drying were a breeze, too.

On Wednesday afternoon, we were herded into the lecture theatre for an input on "policing and society". It was by an outside speaker. The subject matter was so momentous, unbounded and uncomfortable for police training that it had sought specialist assistance from the local academic community in Canterbury to deliver the sessions.

You could tell he was an academic. Those heavy black framed glasses (presumably down to eye strain from all of that reading). His hair was unruly, his shirt open-necked with sleeves casually rolled up, and, to top it all, he was wearing bicycle clips in the classroom. (It might have been another twenty-five years until Katie Melua told us there were nine million bicycles in Beijing, but we knew there was at least one at Christ Church College, Canterbury.)

If ever there was a threat to social order (other than a Hampshire sweater), it stood right there in front of us. Maybe he had imported the bike back after some indoctrination programme in China and was now about to spread the word? Not my appraisal, but the assessment of a few in the room, I thought, as our lecturer was greeted with rows of folded arms and defensive suspicion. This might have just been a response to the term "university lecturer". Later, there were rumours of vegetarianism, as though this somehow cemented the "lefty" evaluations. Personally, I just think he didn't like the chili con carne at lunch.

Mr Keynes stood for two hours and talked. And talked and talked. No notes or prompts. His was the kind of talking that you either engage with or experience as a form of white noise. It was like a comprehension test where paragraphs become increasingly complex and loaded with words you don't recognise until the entire extract might as well be written in Russian. As others grabbed an involuntary post-lunch nap, a few of us remained alert enough to try and follow the interlocking insights this captivating and mind-expanding man shared. We were being exposed to a very different world. We were exposed to a world of ideas.

Like most academics in full flow, Mr Keynes was memorable for being fascinating, enlightening and utterly forgettable. To be fair, it was a university lecture delivered to a non-university audience who had not been briefed that taking notes might be helpful. We didn't have a notebook and pen between us (not at all uncommon in the world of police training at any level then or now).

Mr Keynes continued cycling up to see us for the next three weeks, continuing and developing his multi-stranded discourse. No one told me in the fifth week it was all over. I went to an empty lecture theatre, as devoid of Mr K and his audience as the training centre was of progressive ideas. I was crestfallen. Mr K had been a refreshing break from the rote learning of the course. To a degree, he had brought meaning and context to everything else we had been doing.

Post Keynes, there was a Wednesday afternoon slot to be filled. Next up in the lecture theatre: an input on public order policing. It proved quite a contrast.

A superintendent from the City of London arrived. Blonde-haired and in his mid-forties, he sported a blue blazer, aviator sunglasses and a regimental tie that curved around an over-lunched midriff, suggesting membership of the executive of the Superintendent's Association. He had flannel of two types: his grey trousers and the yarn that rolled out of his mouth.

Selections of amusing anecdotes followed, along with some notable advice on how to surreptitiously repel a persistent protester who has got too close to the policing front line. Should you be in the row behind: face forward, eyes front, smile broadly and give him a hefty dig in the ribs between the two officers standing in front of you, just as a personal hello and declaration of friendly intent. Welcome to the City of London!

His audacious stories were broadly amusing, and his larger-than-life personality seemed to fit his Bow Bells, punchy style of delivery. However, there was also a perturbed atmosphere as students assessed the legality of this "diamond geezers'" "advice".

Later, we established that the centre management had picked up on the "bespoke content" that had seemingly deviated from the policing public order manual, and so the rotund, regimentally attired entertainer was given more time to enjoy future courses, this time of the culinary variety, as his presence on this course came to an abrupt end.

The contrast between university delivery and the methods of learning at the centre was stark. One involved critical thought; the other didn't. There was a lot of law and procedure to take in. Inevitably, the early focus was on basics like the Theft Act. (As an old timer told me back in force, "There are only two offences you need to know to police in the city: Theft and TWC[6].")

Learning law and procedure was achieved by memorising definitions by heart - a very repetitive and boring activity. Evenings and weekends involved rote learning while repetitively yawning through the tedium of it all. It was a hard slog: dull with a capital D, and duller even than a damp day in Dulwich. It even made the thought of a couple of hours out in Ashford town centre faintly appealing.

Failure to learn definitions meant failing the weekly Monday morning test. This led to having to write a "duty report" as to why. This seemed to be a cunning exercise to practice "confession" in discipline investigations back in the real world, where duty reports were required in the first response to a complaint or alleged breach of discipline. How do you explain that you are just a bit thick? Or, more accurately, bored to buggery?

A few weeks in, and I found myself having to explain why I couldn't fully recall the definition of burglary. I was a bit stuck. "Couldn't be arsed" seemed inappropriate. "I was bored to the point of topping myself" looked a little melodramatic. "Sorry, I'll try not to do it again", appeared the safest response.

Knowledge, though, is power, and this is certainly the case in policing. Having a detailed understanding of Acts and sections does help, especially if you have the quickness of mind to be able to apply it to what is unfolding in real-time. However, it seems it isn't vital; student officers these days don't learn like this. I once met an inspector who told me he'd never known what he'd arrested anyone for, he just knew they'd done wrong, and he was confident he'd work it out later at the station.

Police promotion exams require memorising huge tracts of information in the subject areas of crime, traffic and the vast syllabus of general police duties. Many a brightly talented young thing found the exercise impossible and so never rose above the rank of constable. In contrast, a legion of robotic rote learners who

---

[6] Taking a motor vehicle without consent.

dreamt of pips on their pyjamas rose to positions of authority roughly inverse to the luminosity of their personalities.

There was quite a contrast between the idealism of the Keynes monologues and the work of the "duty squad". This was one of the joys of training school: your class being duty squad for the week. The role meant having to maintain site security outside of classroom hours, including weekends, once every four weeks, and therefore being confined to the centre and unable to go home. We would conduct tedious foot patrols of the grounds and buildings, designed to get us used to walking about in our uniforms while carrying a radio and large torch. It was the military equivalent of guard duty and certainly saved the Home Office the cost of private security. Interestingly, during the two-week Christmas break, locked doors and a burglar alarm seemed to suffice.

Another squad task was guarding at the gatehouse, checking vehicles in and out of the site—except those of residents, whom we were under express instructions not to check but to wave through. (There were private homes within the grounds and the residents were, not unsurprisingly, disinclined to be security checked several times daily, as though they lived on the Shankill Road.)

As it was December and the east of England, gate duty could be like standing on the bridge of a frigate in the Baltic Sea: the cutting east wind doing its best to bear snow while frosting facial features. Eventually, it did snow, spectacularly, dumping mounds of it on the final Friday before the great Christmas escape. We only just got out, dodging the cotton white duvet of doom that was blocking roads behind us. It disappeared like a pursuing state trooper as we crossed the county line into Surrey.

There is something very desolate about an institutional setting at weekends. Its emptiness is amplified in contrast to the busyness of its corridors and classrooms during the working week. You feel your isolation, despite the presence of a few others. Time drags, especially when sitting in a stark, cell-like single room trying to learn the law off by heart while waiting to assume the cold drudgery of patrol or gate duty. BBC radio was my saviour from insanity, and on Sundays, I found cheer in listening to a charitable icon that, in retrospect, was a white-haired, cigar-puffing paedophile.

Monday, and everyone's back. It's exam day. Failure can mean "back coursing". One Clacton-on-Sea-bound student made it to week nine before sliding back to week two, like a blue counter in a grotesque game of snakes and ladders.

This time, I made the pass mark along with my classmates and could relax, for now.

To apply the knowledge that we had been digesting (in indigestible chunks), we were set "practicals": exercises designed to translate theory into action.

I was selected to be the lead actor in a short play, which I was unaware was scripted as a farce. In front of my classmates, I found myself in a very dimly lit, disused outbuilding. My helmet struck a beam in the darkness due to my height, and I considered it reasonable to remove it. Wrong decision, constable!

"Put that helmet back on!" barked the angry voice of the course commander, Inspector Stern.

I glanced at him, expecting to see a megaphone, but there wasn't one. He was a humourless individual with the demeanour of a Yorkshire County opening batsman. Off duty, he was a Salvation Army Captain and a mild figure of fun, as an informant had revealed a story from his past.

As a PC dog handler, Stern was called out from bed one night to track burglars. CID and assorted individuals, including the well-to-do and influential householders, waited patiently for him for the best part of an hour. He pulled up in a flurry of blue lights, showering gravel as he skidded to an impressive-looking halt in the driveway of the large house. Having leapt from his van, he threw open the rear doors. At this point, things became somewhat less impressive as it became apparent to all that, in his excitement and rush to get to the scene of the crime, he'd forgotten one important furry thing … the dog. The possessor of a prominent nose on his suitably embarrassed face, one detective dryly enquired whether he might put it to use in order to get some benefit from the situation.

Back in the outbuilding, scolded and flustered, I did as I was instructed. I saw a bundle of rags on the floor. As I approached, it moved in a cloud of muck and dust before forming into the figure of a prone human being who then hugged me around my ankles like I'd just found him on a desert island. The vagrant was none other than Bob the Bell Ringer. I had little interest in his inspired performance as I dejectedly observed the state of my previously immaculate boots. At this point, Bob became less of a bell ringer and more of a bell end to my mind. I dealt with the matter adequately by applying the most up-to-date law applicable: a section inspired by the Napoleonic era's Vagrancy Act of 1824, which was created to protect property from the large number of returning and destitute soldiers. I'm sure cycle-clips-Keynes would have had something to say about its prominence in the training curriculum. My reflections were more prosaic: I spent the evening spitting at a vision of Bob the Bell End on my toe caps until he transformed into a shining vision of me.

Honouring the declared primary role of a constable to protect life, we were required to achieve bronze level in the national life-saving swimming awards. The training centre didn't have its own pool, so each week at 6 a.m., we were up, in full uniform, in the black and cold eastern air to board our transport. The "Green Goddess", as it was affectionately known at the centre, was an ancient wartime relic of a bus with a military lineage dating back to General Gordon by the look of it. The omnibus took us to the local swimming baths early, under cover of darkness, for lifesaving instruction before the unsuspecting public could detect our presence and ponder whether any of us lager lashers from the night before had had a sly pee in the pool. Given the amount of chlorine in the water, someone on the staff had a similar thought.

In the baths, we learned to recover bricks and a technique of rescue where we cupped the chin of the person in difficulty and towed them to safety. This worked well when the rescued person was not flailing about in a blind panic, pushing the rescuer underwater to stay afloat, so we were all confident we could apply it next time there was an issue at the local reservoir. Not.

On Tuesday, the 9th of December, we clambered onto the bus, sitting in a mildly dazed silence as befitted the hour. As the ancient engine spluttered and then burst into life like an ageing Dakota aircraft, Dan bounded onto the vehicle looking decidedly chipper with malevolence in mind. He clapped his gloved hands gleefully as he addressed the assembled class.

"Anyone on here like John Lennon?" he asked chirpily.

There were murmurs of appreciation for the Beatles' musical genius and a generally warm vibe as he stirred our imaginations, and we nodded and mumbled in unison that we did.

"Shame. Someone pumped six bullets into him last night. Imagine that."

Leaving us feeling like we had just witnessed the murderous act, he turned to settle in his chair, beaming with mischievous self-satisfaction. In the rear-view mirror, he could see the shell-shocked souls in the seats behind.

Presumably, that was the "how to deliver a death message" part of the programme covered. It was a subdued trip on what seemed a very long and winding road to the pool. It was a sadly sombre lifesaving lesson that followed. The rest of the day wasn't so good either, except perhaps for delighted Dan.

As you might envisage, there was a lot of classroom work on learning the law. The curriculum had its staples: The Theft Act, The Offences Against the Persons Act, The Sexual Offences Act, and The Animals Act.

Our lesson on obscene language was short. Bob stood in front of the class and said, "I'm going to cover the topic of obscene language; it's fairly brief."

With that, the door opened, and Dan walked in and recited the following: "Mary had a little pig, it wouldn't stop grunting, so she took it down the garden shed and kicked its fucking c**t in!" He then left, shutting the door behind him. There was a shocked and bemused silence.

"Gentlemen, you have now heard the only two words that constitute obscene language in English law. Here endeth the lesson." We were early to lunch that day. For some reason, I ate salad and avoided the pork.

I tended to use the bar on-site as it was more convenient. Socialising was encouraged, and classes normally sat together from nine onwards, the time from which recruits arrived having completed their studying, or from nine-fifteen if a nine o'clock parade had been awarded. There was a dress code of a collared shirt and sports jacket that the bar staff tried to enforce. If they could entice you to wear a tie, all the better as far as they were concerned. Again, it seemed very "military" and very conservative. It was rather like being at a boarding school but without the food fights. Drunkenness was heavily discouraged unless you were a member of staff, in which case it was expected, and you could do it openly and belligerently. The alcoholics, who had asked to be seconded as trainers so they could get away from the strictures of home and have a cheap bar on their doorstep, were hard to control. Fortunately, their performances were generally late evening when exhausted recruits had retired to bed.

As the foundation stones of law were laid down, each day brought more practical scenarios for recruits to simulate real situations. One young PC, who has been a cadet, complained bitterly that "this isn't what happens in the real world," as we debriefed one role play. After being given the opportunity to shut up and tow the party line, he was invited out of the classroom by both tutors, where the party line was forcefully attached to him and his mouth firmly stitched shut by it. He looked scolded, but then he had just had his bell well and truly rung by Bob and Dan.

Outside, shivering in my raincoat and liner combo, I was waiting to do a road traffic accident role play when I saw another class grouped around the front door to a two-story outbuilding being used as a house.

A stout, bottle green sergeant on secondment from the Royal Ulster Constabulary, resplendent in a tall cap bearing a harp on a bright red background, was instructing "C" class in the practicalities of serving a summons. The sergeant was businesslike and unimpressed. His target was a chin-strap-wearing ex-gunner who was as cheery a chap as you could imagine, but with limited practical sense and who was struggling on the course. (He later became a popular beat officer in Bexhill.) He was making a hash of "process serving", and the result was a Belfast blast from the irritated instructor.

"PC Ludlite, you're stupid, so you are." Ludlite looked about, bewildered; the paper summons gripped in his left hand.

"You don't approach a door like that. You're too close. You should be side on. What if someone comes out and tries to stab or shoot you?"

Bexhill might not be Belfast, and The High Street might not be the Falls Road. However, the point was reasonable. Many officers have been badly injured on a doorstep, and not just from tripping over milk.

"Where I'm from, if you stood that close, you'd be likely to get urinated on from the bedroom window. Now do it again."

I could see that, even with a waterproof cover on the flat cap one might be wearing, that kind of shower would be no fun, golden or not.

We were instructed that domestic disputes were potentially volatile and violent and that we must, when we can, attend in pairs. I was in a scenario: a man has found his wife has been cheating. He's been drinking and has a disassembled shotgun on his desk. My job was to deal with the situation.

I was faced with a large, middle-aged, somewhat grizzled sergeant who certainly looked like he was partial to a drop of the hard stuff, so had been well cast. He was difficult and dismissive of my youth as I tried to reason with him as best I could, but he wasn't really responding. At the end of the scenario, Bob was encouraging. Then the thespian supervisor said, "One point, son: you let me assemble the gun."

Good point! I realised I should have intervened before he inserted the cartridge, but I didn't know what my powers were. In real life? Get the gun. The lesson is better learned here than on the job proper. On this occasion, instead of shots being fired, we headed for another high-carbohydrate, low-taste lunch, where the incident was clearly still on my mind, as I negligently discharged an excessive amount of ketchup over my chips.

Another scenario I managed to make a hash of was away from the classroom in a block used exclusively for role play. I was told a traffic accident had occurred and the driver killed. We knew the registered keeper of the vehicle. I managed, in my nervousness, to walk into the trap by informing the registered keeper's wife that her husband was dead. This was unfortunate because he wasn't: someone else was driving the car, but I didn't ask the right questions, and trying to do so, after informing her that her nearest and dearest was in the mortuary, had caused her to clam up tighter than a rectum with rigor mortis. Her grief was my grief, her pain, my pain. Even my pleading that I got the point and that we should pack up and go for tea fell on deaf ears as we sat in feigned silence, wringing every last drop of shame from the situation. It wasn't my last encounter with a difficult death message, assuming there are any easy ones. There are, but you don't know until you've delivered it.

As the weeks progressed, there were lessons on the law regarding dogs and the requirement for registration and collars (with no such corresponding regulation covering the clergy, despite them, arguably, posing a greater risk) and a particularly long double session about vehicle excise licences and the use of trade number plates.

Motor traders applied for "trade plates", which they put on vehicles being test-driven or delivered. The rules were strict. Popping home for lunch wasn't on the list of exempt activities; neither was visiting a golf course for a few holes or, indeed, visiting any premises for a similar or dissimilar recreational purpose. Nipping to the shops for milk in time for afternoon tea at the showroom was a no-no too, and we recruits were instructed to be vigilant towards the possibility of traders "abusing the privilege". This meant that probationary constables, the length and breadth of England and Wales, were routinely stopping cars being delivered on trade plates at just about every opportunity.

One angry and weary delivery driver I was to stop early one morning had five HORTI forms, issued by officers for the production of a driver's licence, insurance and MOT certificate. (The driver had five days to produce, and they were therefore often dubbed "producers" by the public.) The driver had travelled one way from Nottingham and had been stopped by police five times. I was the sixth as he started the hazardous return journey. He'd been on the road for five minutes. Seeing the five HORTIs he already had, I tore up mine, apologised and explained the position. I wished him the best of luck on his journey back. He was going to need it. Little did we both know my good luck quotient expired in less than seven minutes—that was how long it took before a traffic unit pulled him over en route to the motorway. Cringing, I waved sympathetically as I skulked by.

There were other highlights from the curriculum, such as Public Service Vehicles (the regulation of buses). Drivers had to be licensed, of course, and wear their badge in a conspicuous position. My more recent (post-millennial) experience of a local bus driver was noticing the only thing he had in a conspicuous position was a can of soft drink clutched in his right fist as he fought, one-handed, to round a corner. Another was even more contemporary and held the obligatory mobile phone. Perhaps it was her first time on the route.

In 1981, drivers were not allowed to speak to anyone unless it was in the interests of safety. An officious young officer, just out of probation, with a hawk's eye for an offence, was determined to get onto the traffic department. To impress on his selection board and have something to talk about, he reported a driver and conductor on a Southampton corporation bus he had spotted exchanging a joke while their vehicle was moving. I wondered if he reported them for talking or being in possession of a sense of humour: he'd clearly lost his.

Of course, buses were then generally staffed with a driver and conductor duo (like on the hit TV show "On the Buses") and weren't single-crewed. They were also a major part of the transport infrastructure, conveying millions to and from work each day. Local councils ran bus services employing hundreds of workers. Now that has largely gone as services have been privatised. The huge Southampton city bus depot that was is now a supermarket with an extensive taxi rank outside. Progress indeed.

Sudden deaths were inevitably on the list of subjects. As Bob the Bell Ringer told us prophetically, "One minute you're 'ere, next minute you ain't." This was as far as the philosophical reflection went. The most helpful aspect of the procedure was the sensible advice to "check that the person is actually dead". Stories were imparted of bodies being found, detectives arriving, photographers and scenes of crime officers attending, next–of–kin being notified, funerals and flowers arranged, and sandwiches and beer ordered only for the "deceased" to be discovered to be still breathing. Some people are just absolutely determined to never miss a party.

A session called Statutory Preventive Measures was interesting as it was sold as providing a kind of street police toolbox of powers. First was "going equipped to steal", a section of The Theft Act. We were instructed that when a person was away from where he lived and had with him an article for use in any burglary, theft or deception, an offence was committed with a power of arrest. Walking down a city street one night, a young man was stopped by police and found to be carrying a thin plastic shopping bag stuffed into his pocket. Forensic questioning followed. "What's this for, son?"

His reply, "To steal a portable TV from my mate's house," led to the termination of both the questioning and the walk and a trip to a room where a TV was sadly missing. In compensation, there was a toilet in shiny stainless steel and a décor that would today be described as minimalistic.

Sometimes, forensic questioning wasn't needed. A PC stopped a man riding a bike without lights one Christmas Eve. The rider asked, "How did you know it was stolen?"

"I didn't know, but I do now," replied the constable, for whom Christmas really had come early.

Another measure mentioned earlier was the Vagrancy Act. Enacted to deal with the rise in crime from soldiers returning from the Napoleonic wars, it prohibited many things, including pretending to tell fortunes. This might have led to the prosecution of various contemporary tabloid astrologers, but for the get-out clause that to be convicted, you had to have already been convicted as an idle person - merely being one was not sufficient.

The good news was that some of this preventative legislation was repealed in various Acts of Parliament. This hadn't stopped it from being taught to us, though, and of course, it was the practical that led that boot-wrecking bastard Bob to blemish my perfectly shone Doctor Martens.

The offence of burglary, at that time, involved entering a building or part of it with intent to steal, assault, damage or rape. There was a classroom debate one morning over the meaning of enter. We were told the merest part of the body intruding into the premises amounted to an entry, as did the use of an implement; a stick, for example, or a child, or indeed, as Dan pointed out, a monkey. The example was expanded; a monkey sent in to steal amounted to burglary by its owner. As the debate around this intensified, one student officer with a playful, slightly off-the-wall disposition posed the question, "Ok, so this bloke intends to rape. What if he sends the monkey in to do it?"

They are still looking through the law books on that one.

Many people, to the irritation of legal language pedants, say they have been robbed when they haven't: they have been burgled. Robbery is theft with force, so being dragged out of your VW Golf GTI and having it stolen is robbery. Someone breaking into your house and sending a monkey in to steal the family silver is burglary. Getting a monkey to steal a car is theft, along with being a very lucrative circus act.

Our first lesson back in November had been "The Modern Police Service." I thought it ironic. The focus was on Police Regulations and a long list of infractions we could be sacked for. In those days, demotion was a much-used sanction. An unsubstantiated story, from a west country force, told of a detective superintendent reduced in rank to sergeant for loose-tongued behaviour around a woman constable at a fairly rumbustious social function. If you are wondering what it was that he said, the answer is: absolutely nothing. His ability to talk and hear was somewhat restricted by the proximity of her thighs.

It was made clear that, as probationers, we could be fired if it was believed we weren't mentally or physically fit to perform our duties or if it was considered we weren't likely to become "efficient or well-conducted police officers". This was the yardstick against which we were judged. There weren't any lessons on contemporary policing in a modern society other than Mr Keynes's ecologically sustainable inputs. There was nothing on Human Rights or diversity, but then, the first was something people thought related to the United Nations and diversity, as said earlier, hadn't been invented yet. Come to think of it, neither really had Human Rights. They were enshrined in law from just after the Second World War, but they hadn't landed on the consciousness of the service or the populace. It was the nineteen-nineties before this properly impacted. It has been a rocky road ever since, and Human Rights legislation is under attack, and understandably so. I mean, who needs Human Rights? Who needs laws that make the police and public authorities consider the rights of individuals and their families to maintain personal freedoms and a truly free society? While we're at it, why not ditch Magna Carta, all don armbands and be done with it?

I wasn't aware of, and had no reason to consider, the service's attitude to homosexuality. I use that term as it was in use then and seems to have made a bit of a contentious comeback more recently in some quarters.

Back in the early eighties, there was plenty of banter that would have been described as "horseplay" (whatever that is. Bullying?) that would be highly inappropriate today. The TV show "Are You Being Served" had been running since 1972, finishing in 1985. John Inman's comic depiction of a gay department store salesman had a significant impact on the national consciousness and comedic behaviour, and he was regarded with near national treasure status (in a time when national treasure status hadn't been invented). Windsor Davies' alpha male, anti "poofs", army sergeant in the comedy show, "It Ain't Half Hot Mum", was still running and was similarly popular. These and other cultural markers, like Alf Garnett, shaped attitudes and public behaviour.

This was brought home during a lesson on Sexual Offences. We were being taught the offence of gross indecency between males. A mild wind of liberalism had led to a legal change in 1967 that provided a defence where the male participants were; we were told by the instructor, "In private, over 21, only two can play, and there must be free consent." To reinforce this, we were offered a handy mnemonic: "POOF".

How very playfully creative our educators were.

Flash forward almost twenty years to the turn of the century, and my legal knowledge from this time came in very useful. I was sitting in an extremely hot, packed theatre in Edinburgh, at the Fringe. On stage was a very popular comedian at the time called Adam Bloom[7].

"Who knows when homosexuality was legalised?" Adam asked. There followed a lengthy silence.

I, of course, knew and eventually felt duty-bound to offer him the line he was looking for: "67," I shouted out.

Quick as a dawn firing squad on the way to a fried breakfast, he bellowed, "Queer!" pointing his left arm out to the side in my direction without looking at me, much to the mirth of the freely consenting, adult alternative comedy crowd who'd turned out to enjoy his act in sauna-like conditions.

Bet he doesn't use that material now.

Back to 1981, and two members of our intake in another class had a running joke between them where they would "camp" it up at every opportunity. This kind of immature behaviour would get short shrift nowadays, and they'd be out. The organisation would be disappointed they had made it through selection interviews, where questions are set to expose immature or inappropriate behaviours and attitudes. Back then, it was seen as high jinks and banter in line with existing cultural attitudes, as was Adam Bloom's very funny show almost twenty years later. The instructors took little or no notice or didn't see it as comment-worthy. They were, perhaps, still laughing at the mnemonic. Both students were popular and outgoing, with one an outstanding athlete.

Unfortunately for the two officers concerned, their behaviour had been noticed by a group of students on their final probation course, a two-week

---

[7] 1998 Time Out Comedy award winner for best Stand-Up.

training module delivered around eighteen months of service, just before final confirmation of appointment.

These probationary "old sweats" were a jaded, alcohol-sodden, bitter bunch. Their hate conjured up The Jam's song, "Down in a Tube Station at Midnight", as they indeed smelt of pubs, maybe not of Wormwood Scrubs, but certainly of malicious right-wing meetings (whatever they smell of). A few seemed unimpressed by the antics of their junior colleagues; not because they thought it inappropriate, insensitive or offensive, but rather on the grounds of group homophobia, mixed with self-importance and faux outrage, as far as I could tell.

The situation worsened when the duo inadvisably decided to perform a highly camp, comically risky version of the "Sugar Plum Fairy" at the week seven entertainment night. Each class was obliged to provide some form of "entertainment" for other students and staff. Had they just been performing to their course they would have been fine. However, present in the bar that night was the sour-natured, intoxicated group who wanted to project their bile onto something or someone.

The pink fairy, resplendent in wings with a silver wand, fluttered across the stage to groans from the line of malcontents propping up the counter. The selected fairy jokes fell flatter than the beer. However, it was the joke that took the mickey out of the final probation course that raised their ire to malevolently venomous levels. The next morning, an official complaint was laid, and the camp commandant investigated.

The upshot was that, as our class did a practical in the lower car park near the training centre exit, an open-top MG sports car flew down the drive, suitcase visible in the rear. We gazed on with alarm as the sugar plum fairy passed us, making a pronounced thumbs-down sign as he did so. We were shocked and angry. He was a popular, likeable guy. As far as we knew, he was being kicked out because he was suspected of being gay. Why? His classmate managed to stay, but it was reportedly a close call. It was said that being married saved him.

Later, there was a sense of smug, spiteful satisfaction among those who had got him dismissed. Today, he would have met the same fate earlier, but for entirely different reasons. This wouldn't be the last time I would witness homophobia in the next few months.

Things are now much improved across the service in England and Wales (which comprises 43 *separate forces*).[8] The 2023 Casey Report on the Met Police, though, makes worrying reading.[9]

One objective of the course was to get recruits fitter, presumably to equip them with the ability to chase burglars. In some cases, it was simply to enable them to walk without perspiring excessively. With no fitness standard to be achieved before joining, there was some disparity between the fittest and the "fit for fuck alls". With my fitness on arrival at Ashford decidedly average, I was at least skinny, and the gym regime started to help, along with the seven-mile runs that we had three times over the ten weeks. From a lumbering start, I found a sprint finish in the second run, propelling me to sixteenth: not bad considering I put on a stone in weight, elevating me to twelve stone six pounds. This, at least, meant I was less likely to be blown away like an empty black bin liner when walking the beat in a strong wind. In the final run during week eight, I jogged to the line in a respectable second place. As the winner was also from "A" class, we cleaned up on the trophies.

Similarly, in the five-a-side competition, we prevailed in a tense final where, after Cleve the Herculean scored a thunderous shot, I had the satisfaction of scoring the winner. From the sidelines, Peter Pool observed that you could see the effort we had individually expended by the grass stains on our kit and knees. I glanced down and saw mine (both knees and kit) were conspicuously white. I could have folded my shorts and put them back in the drawer. Still, work smarter, not harder, they say. I got a small plastic trophy as my reward. Just as well. I never got another for any sporting activity—ever. I had peaked.

Towards the end of the course, after the final exam, I began to panic. I had been attending evening lessons put on by the Supplementary Training Unit for those in need of remedial intervention. Some attendees were self-doubters like me, while others were present through the fear of "back coursing" or ejection from the programme altogether. Sat, reeking of "the great smell of Brut" splash on lotion, I failed to realise that the absence of women in the seats around me and my selection of fragrance might be inextricably linked.

---

[8] Several have featured in the Stonewall top 100 LGBTQ+ employers in recent years: four in 2020; 1 in 2023.
[9] Baroness Casey Review: Final Report: An independent review into the standards of behaviour and internal culture of the Metropolitan Police Service March 2023.

The STU helped—spectacularly. I went from writing duty reports explaining my memory lapses to grades that put me in the running for top student. The idea of that filled me with dread. Not the thought of coming first, but more the consequence. As top student, you had to make a speech at the final course dinner in front of all staff, students and distinguished guests. I'd found introducing myself to the class an ordeal; I was, therefore, mortified at the prospect, which was becoming a distinct possibility.

After the exam, Dan and Bob entered the classroom bearing a sheet of paper. There was an expectant silence. My armpits were clammy under my tunic. My heart was racing.

"We have a top student amongst us, gentlemen," declared Dan as though announcing the presence of a spy.

He then called out the final exam results. I was first in the class with ninety-two percent. All eyes swung towards me, and one student pointed accusingly as though identifying a paedophile in a playground (although paedophiles hadn't been invented yet).

"So, Mr Roach is top student!"

I was dropped like a drug-taking defender at Doncaster Rovers, as all eyes swung away from me like I was yesterday's news. They fell on the opposite side of the room, where Dave was now the headline story and looking more surprised than anyone, despite his obvious hard work. He had scored second in the final exam, but his more consistent performance across the ten weeks had relegated me to runner-up, and I could not have been more overjoyed. I was flooded with relief, as though I had just been pardoned. It meant I only had the job of saying grace in two sentences and then sitting down. Dave had to sing for his supper.

With first and second places in the exam, along with our sporting successes, the class enjoyed a glory that, in our minds, was near Olympian. These results had been the culmination of a team effort over ten weeks, where we had dragged one another along with good cheer (and plenty of beer) and where even the weakest swimmers got their bronze lifesaving award. We could now all render basic first aid and had become particularly adept at diagnosing wrist and arm injuries; due mainly to the number inflicted by the self-defence trainer on the occasions where, after throwing one of us mercilessly to the mat, he had applied various oriental arm holds that no one could imagine using with any degree of proficiency.

The rest of the week breezed by as I helped Dave with his speech. The dinner was on a Thursday night: the day before the passing out parade and our release on probation from custody.

At dinner, I found myself sitting in the middle of the other top table, or the bottom table, to be more precise. Opposite me, across the dining hall, about forty place settings away, sat Dave. It was a boring and lonely place to be, and if it felt like command for a moment, then maybe it was better to be at the bottom, as while my classmates laughed and joked, I made tedious small talk with an insipid inspector to my left and a colourless county counsellor to my right.

Fervently rehearsing my supporting act in my head, I eventually got it out and off my shoulders. Rather than the unofficial school version of, "In your mouth and round your gums, look out stomach here it comes", I manage to force out, "For what we are about to receive..." pretty faultlessly. At least I could enjoy the food now, which was more than could be said for Dave. I knew nothing of wine, but of that supplied, I concluded it would be a good accompaniment for chips, which, sadly, were not on the menu.

Dave's speech was witty and entertaining. He used my description of Dan Sower as being the epitome of a "course sergeant". It was bullseye accurate, although there was a slight pause before the double meaning penetrated the collective consciousness of the partially sloshed crowd and raised a laugh. The obligatory end-of-course "disco" followed, resembling perhaps an event put on by the young conservatives, but with more beer. Punk rock or anything vaguely anti-establishment was noticeably absent from the playlist, but Abba got a headline airing.

In the morning, we were each given an end-of-course chat by Bob and Dan. Disconcertingly, they gently suggested I should perhaps be in some other field of endeavour. It seemed my ability to say grace competently, combined with an interest in the thoughts of Chairman Keynes, had skewed their perceptions.

Later, white-gloved and gleaming after the passing out parade on that cold but clear and crisp Friday, I baulked at paying £3.50 for a post-parade photograph, the artistic angle of which gave a clear view up my left nostril. (The photographers did a magnificent job in developing the pictures in this pre-digital age before students left the site.)

Being 1981, the American college and military tradition of throwing headgear into the air had not infected the national student consciousness yet, which was just as well, as a flurry of descending helmets would likely have led to an alarming level of head and neck compression injuries.

There followed emotional farewells between us all before we each walked up to Dan and Bob, shook hands and said a final goodbye. Both had guided us through the ten weeks with energy, inventiveness, kindness (Bob only) and humour (much of it very black). Something had ended that was significant and which we all recognised we would miss. We were their best class ever (I bet they say that to all the boys).

It had been an intensely formative, emotionally shared experience that probably everybody who completes a course of extended residential training of this type feels in one way or another. Some students loitered, seemingly reluctant to leave and give up the security of the centre with its framework, focus and fun. I had mixed emotions, but it was over. The centre itself held no real attraction to me and, as my case was already stowed in the car, I ran down the drive with Alex from where, like escaped convicts, we hit the high road west to freedom.

4 Local Procedure Course

The next two weeks were like heaven. After a few days off, I met up with my small gang of Hampshire colleagues. We were on a local procedure course; essentially a form-filling fortnight. It was February: the skies were a clear azure blue, with a dazzling frost topping the fields surrounding the Victorian school building in Bishop's Waltham. This had been the now-defunct police cadet training school and was now used for force training.

The cadet scheme had allowed forces to recruit sixteen-year-old police officer hopefuls and occupy them until they were old enough to join as constables at eighteen and a half. The idea was that it kept these youngsters engaged in self-developmental activities; otherwise, on leaving school at sixteen, they would go into other work and be lost to the service.

Due to the epic recruitment shortages of the seventies, the scheme was important, indeed vital. The cadet programme involved, amongst other things, voluntary service, a bit of additional education through college day release, work experience in police stations, lots of physical activity (including muddy cross-country runs) and, of course, lots of military-style discipline: shoe shining, marching, folding bedding into bed packs, parading, inspections and having your hair shorn to crew cut level (boys only of course).

Sometimes a cadet would get to accompany an officer on patrol. On these occasions, they were generally not at all welcomed with any enthusiasm by regular officers, who accorded them roughly equal status to special constables (or "hobby bobbies" as they were rather cruelly dubbed). One excited young cadet, waiting for his turn in the area car at Havant police station, was checking his appearance in a full-length mirror when he was summoned by the driver with the less than fraternal greeting of, "Alright, come on then wanker. No one's going to be looking at you anyway." Apparently, it kind of took the lustre off the experience.

Cadets spent their final year overseas as the ultimate exercise in personal development (it also meant the instructors didn't have to devise activities to keep them amused for yet another twelve months). It was also a natural exit point, as by that time, most had had sex with just about everyone they fancied, and some they didn't, so it was time to move on.

The overseas assignments were diverse and could be challenging, like "working" in a sailing school in Hong Kong, rounding up sheep in the arid Australian outback or shitting on a sand dune in Sudan in front of a bus load of locals, most of whom had never seen a white person before, let alone a white arse the size of a small moon. All of this was done in the pursuit of personal development and, in the latter case, in the pursuit of teaching English as a second language and getting some real "life experience", of which lesson number one was, apparently, shit before you get on the bus.

Some saw the cadet scheme as the salvation of the service. As a bonus, cadets tended to be mega motivated. Some were genuinely outstanding. One gained the Duke of Edinburgh Gold Award and then got a Commendation from the Governor of the Falkland Islands for saving children from a fire during his Voluntary Service Overseas. Later, he won the Lions Club Youth of the Year Award, then promptly donated the £500 winning bursary to a camp for underprivileged children: pretty impressive stuff[10].

Unfortunately, the cadet scheme[11] fell foul of two things: a boom in recruiting after the Edmund Davis pay rise and government cuts, leading to its cancellation

---

[10] More followed as cadet Ian Readhead would eventually become deputy chief constable.

[11] There is now a National Volunteer Cadet scheme. It's not designed as a recruitment feed but to encourage citizenship, voluntary service and a spirit of adventure. It doesn't extend to North African bus rides or sheep shearing in New South Wales.

across the country. It wasn't without its critics, who argued the youngsters were too institutionalised and were, therefore, too narrow in outlook. It's true that some could have easily met the criteria for membership of a right-wing youth movement, but then they simply gravitated towards the traffic department as a form of spiritual home and generally seemed quite settled. The scheme was, though, genuinely important in keeping a steady stream of recruits flowing, and there were plenty of cadets who never lost that childlike buzz of excitement for policing throughout their service. How many people can boast that in their jobs?

We were the only group in the training school, and the atmosphere was as quiet as a church on a Monday. Serene and relaxed, it was a world away from Ashford. There was delicious coffee in tall stainless-steel pots and complimentary newspapers.

The working days mainly involved form-filling Hampshire style, as we were walked through the process of completing road traffic accident reports, sudden death paperwork (called a form G28) and the found dog register. A detective sergeant instructor told us about the most important form in the police service, in his opinion: the sheet that recorded detections. He then thought a bit more and hurriedly amended his hierarchy, demoting the detection sheet to third place behind the expenses form and annual leave card.

The schedule was offset with a touch of light drill on what had been a playground. The drill was nothing compared to Ashford. We also had PE to keep us in fighting fit condition. In the evenings, we sat giggling in local pubs, the stone-floored Crown mainly, enjoying what was a fortnight of rest and recuperation in a gentle, scenic and tranquil county town. I had never been to this part of Hampshire before, and I was taken with its beauty.

We had all been told our postings around week seven at Ashford and were busy discussing them. I was delighted to be going to Shirley, a modern, exciting city station in Southampton (now an even more modern, if less exciting, Lidl). It wasn't exactly "Fort Apache the Bronx", but it looked very exhilarating. And it was.

Alex Peaceman, who was an army bandsman before becoming an electrician, had been posted to the city centre station in Portsmouth. We decided to visit our respective stations for a recce on the mid-Sunday of the course before returning to the training school, so we'd know where to go on our initial duty. We set off for Portsmouth Central first.

I walked in behind Alex, up to the enquiry counter in the cramped, depressingly dark-wooded front office, which was the corporate face of Portsmouth Police. A plain, ponytailed woman in her late twenties who led with her chin looked at my companion unsmilingly and said in an unhelpful tone, "Can I help you?" Tentatively, Alex introduced himself with a wan smile.

'Err, PC Peaceman. I start here in two weeks…'

"You'll want to know your duties then," she declared, interrupting him. She consulted a clipboard hanging behind her among a multitude of papers; some so old and yellowed they could have been issued by the war office and countersigned by Churchill. One warned of the dangers of Colorado beetle, sporting a helpful mug shot of the offender.

"You are nights, starting Monday." She regarded him with an 'anything else you want to bother me with' look.

Alex replied, "Is, is that it? I've come all this way just for that?"

"Didn't they teach you to use the telephone at training school?"

Welcome to Portsmouth.

For six months, Alex walked the beat without the hint of being allowed to travel in a police car. As a probationer on that particular shift, he was relegated to walking by the gutter (if not actually in it) for his full two years. It was also his job to make the tea for the shift and take all the worst jobs, at least until a more junior probationer arrived.

Alex had been placed in the fortress-like police station in Fareham, a few miles out of the city, with a residential room above the dog kennels and next to a hairy and disagreeable PC, whose smuggled-in girlfriend regularly augmented the cacophony of a dog's chorus that assailed his ears each night. It was cumulatively too much for his sensitivities, and he resigned, thoroughly demoralised, joining the family veterinary supplies business, where he got more satisfaction than would be otherwise expected by supplying drugs for the dispatch of unwanted canines. (A bit like aspects of policing: somebody's got to do it.)

Alex's dejection at his reception was somewhat amplified by mine. Travelling back west that Sunday afternoon, we parked in an almost deserted Shirley High Street, straight as the Royal Mile, only longer looking. The sole pedestrian was an ageing, prickly-looking copper ambling up the road towards the station, no doubt in pursuit of refreshments or possibly retirement. He certainly wasn't capable of being in pursuit of anything else. His pullover was stretched way beyond the manufacturer's specification, encapsulating a gargantuan gut that swung from side to side like a huge pendulum and which wouldn't have looked out of place on a pregnant porcupine. Bracing all this was an ancient, straining leather belt. It occurred to me that if a legless man had committed a robbery in front of him, it would have been odds on for the offender to get away.

Concerned at the potential greeting I was about to get, I nevertheless strode confidently up to the police station enquiry counter. Again, a woman was the station duty officer. This time, however, there was a considerably less misanthropic disposition. She beamed at me with sparkling blue eyes as she asked what she could do for me. I explained I was joining the station soon. She quickly explained the shift system and then, without being asked, took a downcast Alex and me on a tour of the station from bottom to top, showing me where I would parade, the lockers, and even where to park. She really couldn't have been more helpful or kind. To finish it all off, my new shift was just coming on duty, so there was a quick introduction to my patrol sergeant, a very affable and likeable former traffic motorcyclist. It was a very good day: for me, at least.

5 Parented Patrol

Toward the end of the first week at Shirley, I was introduced to my tutor constable. This was the person who would "show me the ropes" for at least the first ten weeks of my service. It was every probationer's goal to be certified as fit for independent patrol by the end of this time frame, which could be extended if the officer was proving to be a "slow learner". To have the tutoring period extended was unusual, and if it happened, the probationer concerned would be regarded as the runt of the litter and have a higher likelihood of failure and dismissal. Independent patrol at ten weeks was a benchmark of competence, and we all knew it.

Tutor constables completed a training course for the role and, although often, like mine, not long out of probation themselves, enjoyed a degree of status in the role, as though it validated their level of professionalism and sense of self. Older sweats, who might have been more proficient in street skills, tended to avoid the job as it involved writing reports and having "a learner" attached to you like an inquisitive puppy, only house-trained.

My tutor was a short, straight-haired 25-year-old blonde called Sue Barker. This inevitably drew a bit of Mickey-taking, generally around her ability in court. Although bright and competent, Sue's heart wasn't fully in policing as, in the last few months, she had found herself an Italian boyfriend. The conversations we had seemed to revolve around Milan, Italian male virility (high), Italian male work ethic (not so high—he was inactively looking for a job). Personally, I just felt the poor guy only had so much energy to go around.

This Italian love match involved a mutual love of food. Eating what he ate, in the 10 weeks Sue worked with me, she expanded as though connected to a foot pump, to the point that she probably had to make an appointment with uniform stores to ease her breathing difficulties. By the time I met Alphonso, he resembled less the lithe Latin lothario of her pocketbook picture but more an overstuffed bell pepper in his red jacket and mop of dark curls above a friendly, good-natured, pre-paternal face.

With a life in northern Italy confirmed, Sue was to leave for a future that seemed to me to amount to an existence of pasta, puke, puree and poo.

On our first shifts together, we patrolled at regulation pace, either up Shirley High Street along a beat known as Main Road North or down Shirley High Street, known, not unsurprisingly, as Main Road South. Although not trained in regulation walking, it seemed to equate to about two and a half miles an hour, less a walk, more of a measured stroll. To walk too fast simply meant getting to the end of the street quicker and having to turn round again if it was the end of your beat. It also meant getting uncomfortably sweaty. Walking in a measured way imparted a degree of bearing while allowing for the scanning of vehicles to find various minor infractions of the law to pursue.

Ask the public if they want to see more police on the streets, and the answer is very often "yes". I often wonder why. If you flood the streets with police, they will find offences. If there's one cop out there, you'll get the work of one cop. Put ten out, and you'll get the work of ten. That PC you lobbied your parish councillor for might just spot your consumptive exhaust or those tyres you just can't part with, even when they are now more suited to Formula 1.

The bobby on the beat at this time had an iconically British feel, providing public safety and security in an accessible, discreet and unarmed way. This latter point holds true today and is taken for granted, yet it is nothing short of astonishing. Of course, actually seeing a patrolling constable these days is a rarity; almost as rare as actually getting the police to answer the phone.

My shift would regularly parade a dozen or more officers. One New Year's Eve, with leave cancelled, I counted 23 police officers on duty for a night turn at Shirley. This included the ABOs (area beat officers) who worked alongside our shift pattern and a couple of special constables. We are now in a position where some *counties* are unlikely to have hugely more than that number on patrol duty at night, let alone one shift in one station in one part of one city.

Off the main road, Sue and I strolled along quiet residential side streets, examining car tax discs to see if any were out of date. We scrutinised the registration numbers as well, and occasionally, there would be evidence of fraud. This was like winning a top prize at the bingo. The frauds would be laughable these days: registration numbers erased and replaced with white paint used for typing errors, and a new registration number inserted. Occasionally, the "criminal" (owner) had gone to the bother of typing the index number in replacement; more often than not, it was just lamely handwritten in biro. In these cases, the car was usually parked in the street outside the owner's address. Enquiries would follow that might lead to arrest. Often, the owner simply couldn't afford the tax, didn't use the car, and didn't have anywhere else to keep it other than on the road.

One evening, I pulled a householder out of his front room from watching Coronation Street as his car was "failing to display" a VEL (vehicle excise licence). The man was utterly frantic, throwing pieces of paper into the air as he searched the tired and untidy Triumph to no avail for the disc he testified to possessing. He was in such a state of angst that I told him I believed his story and wished him a good night. It was my view that the people who were fearful of the police to that degree were almost certainly rule-abiding. I didn't like seeing anyone so scared. He must have mistaken me for a bus inspector. (On the Isle of Wight, one almost threw me off a bus as a young child for failing to produce my ticket. I was too embarrassed to confess to having eaten it.) Back at the station, I mentioned my benevolence to a four-year veteran PC. He was cynically unimpressed. "Bet he hasn't got one," he adjudicated contemptuously. He was, of course, absolutely right.

Informed about an obscure book of Southampton City bylaws, I managed to get hold of a copy in a mission to expand my legal armoury so I could prosecute "The Queen's Business" for minor offences. There was a by-law making it an offence to repair a vehicle on a road. This offence was probably drafted at a time when very few people had cars. Maybe it was designed to stop car owners from frightening the horses. Anyway, by the early eighties, there were plenty of vehicles on the roads, not just being driven but parked, as many city homes were terraced and simply didn't have garages.

Out patrolling, we spotted a car with all four wheels missing. On this occasion, it was not a crime scene. It was sitting up on jacks, parked on the street between a skip and a pile of builder's sand. A couple of days later, it was, unsurprisingly, still there and, therefore, a catalyst for police action. My tutor's instruction, in between regaling me with the recipe for a particularly fine minestrone, was to identify the owner and report for summons.

Like a trainee bloodhound, I obediently sought him out. As the car was parked outside his house, it wasn't an Ellery Queen moment of dogged detective daring. Cautioning the poor man that he did not have to say anything unless he wished to do so, he replied, somewhat exasperatedly, "Well, where the hell am I supposed to repair my car?"

It was a fair question and one I couldn't answer. He was right: where was he supposed to repair it? Of course, it's all very easy to tell someone to take it to a garage, but garages were then, as they are now, expensive, and the majority of people's incomes simply didn't extend to being able to pay for repairs. I couldn't have afforded one myself. Having done my business on behalf of the Crown, I slinked away feeling like a right hypocritical bastard. I can only hope the council regarded this by-law infraction with the contempt it deserved and binned the report.

I had been issued a long black plastic folder shaped like a fixed penalty ticket, which I could keep inside my tunic. Constables were expected to issue a minimum of three fixed penalty notices a month. There were no quotas, please understand, just this reasonable "expectation." So, not only were there traffic wardens deployed to enforce parking violations, but there was also an army of police officers, mainly probationers, doing the same thing. These were dangerous days if you were a motorist, driving or not.

It felt a bit dangerous to me. I didn't like writing tickets as it made me quite nervous. I would shake a little and perspire. I realised my discomfort was from the sense that I was being a sneaky git. (A feeling I tend to have towards traffic wardens today.) I felt like I was doing something wrong and didn't want to be caught in the act. I didn't particularly like confrontation and didn't want some irate owner running over while I was in the process of fixing a plastic bag-covered ticket to their windscreen wiper. Really, what I needed to do was to strengthen my "inner persecutor". (Rest assured, I eventually did.)

As soon as darkness fell, there was an opportunity to stop cars with lights out. This was another way for a constable to generate "process",[12] and, as a probationer, it was important to provide a reasonable flow of this to satisfy supervisors. There was no shortage of cars with lone headlights or side lights not working, driving up and down Shirley High Street, given it was a main thoroughfare into the city.

I would step into the road waving a torch to flag a driver down, all the while hoping I would be visible, given my uniform was the colour of asphalt. Sometimes it was a close call. The stop would often lead to a check of the car for "construction and use" offences. These were all things relating to a vehicle's condition. Vehicles were inspected by torchlight, particularly around the wheel arches. Finding bald tyres was seen as the top offence, as each carried three penalty points, and of course, defective tyres are dangerous. Some of these certainly were, being not just devoid of tread but also rubber, with exposed, bulging lumps of white cord protruding like a particularly prominent inguinal hernia.

Lots of cars around this time were old and prone to corrosion, especially, it seemed, if they were Italian (rumours abounded of corroded steel being forced upon Italian manufacturers by their government). There was certainly no shortage of cars being driven around with sharp panels edged with uneven lines of rust that would have acted like a sabre against any unfortunate pedestrian they struck. Duct tape and patchy filler were often in evidence, effectively holding some cars together.

There was also what was known as a "moving traffic offence". Speeding was one, as was driving without due care or reasonable consideration. Other moving driving offences were more obscure, like having a defective light. It wasn't related to the driver's fitness to drive, but it did mean that the driver could be breath tested.

---

[12] Process was the policing term used to describe minor road traffic related offences and other minor matters which were regarded as non-crime.

I gave my first test after Sue stopped a car close to the police station, around half ten in the evening, for what she described as "overtaking on the nearside". Both the driver and I thought it was passing a vehicle turning right, but she was insistent that a moving traffic offence had taken place and that a breath test should follow. The driver was quite amenable to being tested and affable throughout: that is, until he tested positive. At this juncture, he developed a strop of monumental proportions, being thoroughly difficult throughout the entire process, which in those days involved arrest and the calling out of a doctor to take blood samples for laboratory analysis. Having doubted my birth was valid in the eyes of the church, he proceeded to tell the police surgeon where he could stick his needle. The doctor, with some aplomb, responded coolly that, generally, a suppository would be deemed sufficient in that area and that his time would be better used sticking the needle in the detained person's arm. It wasn't a pleasant experience for any of us.

My next effort was somewhat different. We saw a car with a headlamp out beside a "spud-u-like" outlet. The driver was about forty, with a huge head and a hairstyle later rendered fashionable by the horse racing journalist John McCririck. I told him I required him to provide a specimen of breath for a breath test. He agreed, and I started to assemble the test kit.

The kits were thin green plastic boxes containing a bag, a mouthpiece and a tube containing the crystals that had to be blown through. I assembled the mouthpiece, tube and bag and handed it to the driver. He gave a good impression of blowing, but nothing was happening inflation-wise. Often, drivers blew in such a way that their breath escaped from the corners of their mouths in a vain effort to subvert the procedure. Sternly, I said, "You're not blowing. You need to blow steadily until I tell you to stop."

Again, the man appeared to blow, seemingly making a great effort, but the bag remained completely flat. Getting irritated now at his obvious attempts at perverting the course of justice, I said to him more firmly, "You're not blowing. You must blow hard and steadily into the bag until I tell you to stop. If you fail to do that, you will be arrested." *That told him.*

The fellow then blew with every ounce of breath in his body as though he was trying to inflate a Zeppelin. If he had, it would have gotten off the ground. As the pressure built up behind the still limp bag, his head started to turn a disconcerting hue of red and purple, with a previously unnoticeable vein standing out on his right temple like a beanstalk.

Again: nothing. Fearing the poor man's head was about to explode and make a fearful mess of the surrounding shop fronts, I told him to stop. I took the bag and held it in front of the one good headlamp. The beam shone through the tube of crystals, which looked exactly the colour they did when I took them out of the kit. I then removed the mouthpiece from one end of the glass file and the bag from the other. It was at this point I determined the nub of the problem: *me*. I had failed to break the glass ends off the tube. As a consequence, no air was ever going to pass through the crystals and into the bag, even if the driver had attached an industrial pump to the mouthpiece.

There was a small saw supplied in the casing for the purpose of removing the two tiny, bulbous ends of the glass phials before assembly. Suitably mortified, and with all the faux dignity I could muster, I returned to the driver, who did not smell of alcohol or show any sign of intoxication and told him that the equipment appeared to be defective (as opposed to the officer), and so on this occasion, I was magnanimously giving him the benefit of the doubt. By now, he was just a light shade of pink, and the vein had diminished to a point that I felt a cardiac arrest had less than a fifty percent chance of occurring. On receiving my decision, he displayed the relief of a punter who'd just located a winning lost betting slip. I like to think that when he got home, he enjoyed his King Edward with baked beans and that it really was the spud he liked. Somehow, I doubt it, though.

The police surgeons called out in the early hours to take blood from those arrested for drunk-driving offences were treated like gods, and as a result, some acted like them. Some station sergeants would have everything prepared: documents filled out and phials labelled to shave seconds off the doctor's time, so the medic could simply come in, check there was consent, take the blood, inject it into two small glass containers, sign a couple of documents and then sign the most important document of the night: The Doctors' Fees Book. I seem to recall the fee for five minutes of work was a little over fifty pounds. Police surgeons made a very good living from these callouts. On a busy night, some of them would be up for most of the shift, going from one police station to another around the county. Then it was a quick kip, coffee and off to morning surgery to deal with more pressing matters, like hernias and haemorrhoids.

There was a pretty clear distinction between traffic "process" work and crime investigations. Like oil and water, the two departments of Traffic and CID didn't really mix. Probationers were, of course, expected to learn how to deal with both categories of offences. A fairly routine introduction to crime investigation normally came through dealing with shoplifters. There was a steady but not excessive number at Shirley, which presented quite a mix of policing experience, as opposed to Southampton Central, where a constable's life revolved around processing a daily dose of shoplifters and drunks. The kind of experience a probationer got would very much depend on where they were posted. An officer posted to Ventnor on the Isle of Wight said that one winter, the station didn't record any "in messages" from the public *in four months.* Or put another way, that was four months of everybody doing sod all. Even in London, officers stationed in the centre have a vastly different and generally more boring experience than those in outlying suburban hubs, where the work is more varied. The novelty of drunks, thieves and disorientated tourists soon wears off.

With shoplifting offences, police were generally sent to the manager's office, where the offender was detained, usually by a store detective. Several stores had one-way mirrors allowing staff to observe shoplifters surreptitiously.

There was no discretion when it came to theft. Palming a packet of powdered plaster from a DIY superstore got you arrested. Pocketing a pork pie from the local pastry emporium, found you in a cell. Thereafter, a lengthy interview followed, delving into all aspects of the points to prove under the Theft Act. Then the prisoner would be fingerprinted and photographed. Due to perishability, the exhibits were usually kept by the shop, as the Crime Property Store at the police station was ill-equipped to accommodate a frozen leg of lamb, even if it was "best evidence".

Charge sheets were handwritten, and lengthy shopping lists had to be transposed in long hand: four cans of Heinz baked beans, 1 x packet of Walls sausages, 2 x bottles of Smirnoff vodka, 10 x Whiskas (chicken in jelly) and so forth; the list might run on considerably. At the end, I realised why that "O" level in maths was considered handy: the officer in the case had to add up the combined haul and attribute a value to it, then read out the charge or shopping/shoplifting list to the suspect. The pressure was on while writing the charge sheet, as copies went to the court and on the file. Spelling errors were not acceptable. Neither was illegible handwriting. An officer's biro-busting nightmare was a full trolley of stolen items, each different.

I got the reputation of being a bit of a liberal when I started doing things differently. The police were often called to a large Sainsbury's supermarket at Lordshill, where suspects often stole the odd item, like frozen faggots or fish paste, in among a much larger weekly shop; the remainder of which they paid for. In the store, I'd check if the detained person was suitable for a caution. If there were no previous convictions, I would interview in the manager's office, never taking possession of the goods or the suspect. It was an efficient approach. My only problem was fingerprinting. I had to trust the offender would show up at the station for that, as I couldn't force them because they weren't under arrest. They all showed up, very grateful not to be arrested. One nervous, dark-haired young housewife was beside herself with relief at the discretion of this process, as she was genuinely scared her husband would hit her if he found out. She had purloined Shippam's Salmon spread, and I'm sure it was for her slap-happy husband's sandwiches. Some colleagues were less than impressed. PC Robert Wrench told me these people were thieves and *deserved* arrest. For him, this was part of the punishment process. I disagreed on the latter point and stuck to my liberal principles. Their revenge? They nicknamed me Jeremy Thorpe.

    Other accompanied tasks in those first weeks were dealing with Road Traffic Accidents (RTAs), drunks, and the serving of summonses and warrants. Whether one dealt with a sudden death (known in the trade as a G28 after the form we used) depended on factors somewhat outside one's control.

RTAs were dealt with differently then than now. Today, the police tell you to exchange names and addresses and are unlikely to attend unless it involves a serious injury. In 1981, if the police were told about an accident, they would attend, assess culpability, and report offenders for "process". Accident scenes were chalk-marked, measurements taken from fixed points, and then rudimentary diagrams created to allow for the scene to be re-created (I never saw one that was). There was a whole industry around this.

    Witness statements were taken, and suspects interviewed under caution, with notes usually recorded in the officer's notebook. As a certain pedantic training school traffic instructor had told us, "There's no such thing as a Road Traffic Accident. Every incident is somebody's fault. If it weren't, it wouldn't have happened." These were people with a black-and-white outlook you really couldn't argue with. It would be like arguing with a terrorist or a member of the National Rifle Association. Anyway, somebody somewhere in Whitehall must have been a music lover and, listening to Elvis Costello's "Accidents Will Happen", decided to ease the police out of all that paperwork and that nit-picking industry and give the public a break. Over to the insurers.

One evening, with my tutor on a night's leave, I found myself going out on patrol with the acting sergeant: a breezy, braces-wearing Portsmouth lad who would later be bitten by the bug of ambition and wish for waitress service. In the meantime, he was going out with me on patrol in a panda car.

On this occasion, the panda was not an all-white Ford Escort saloon but the last of the real pandas, a blue-bodied white doored mini, soon to be scrapped. In my view, a tad too late, as, at almost six feet four in height (I was still growing), I had to fold up like a lock knife to wedge myself into a space smaller than a microwave oven. The acting sergeant believed in wearing hats in police vehicles. He was OK, as his was a flat cap and he was of average height. I, however, was wearing a helmet and therefore forced to adopt a position where the rim nestled on my knees like I was a combination of a praying mantis and the PC character from Hattytown Tales[13], whose helmet extended down to his thighs. Getting out of the mini in anything like a hurry was not going to happen. Ideally, I should have called in a crane to haul me out. However, in my youth, I was sufficiently pliable to be able to put both palms on the pavement and cantilever my frame as though erecting a marquee at a village fete. Dignified it was not.

I had a summons to serve, so we drove to the address on a small council estate (with seven in the city, it seemed most addresses we visited were rented out by the corporation). I knocked on the door. A weary, middle-aged man wearing a string vest and holding half a smouldering cigarette answered. In my best training school delivery, I served the summons with the precision and authority of a minor town crier. I stood side-on, back from the door and glanced upwards for open windows and any sign of an Ulster greeting. The recipient looked at me like he thought I was an idiot. Unconvinced that I knew this, he decided to eliminate any ambiguity.

"Why can't you just roll up and say, 'Hey mate, I've got a bleedin' summons here for you', without all of that?"

And there I was, thinking I was being all "professional". Note to self: that doesn't mean you have to be a ruddy robot, Brian.

As part of my introduction to "F" division, I had to see the top bosses on separate occasions. Both had offices located at Southampton Central. The first was with the divisional commander[14], a square-jawed Geordie who was forthright and business-like. He stated he hoped I remained clean-shaven as there were too many macho moustaches in the force. He also ended with an entry from the modern

---

[13] Children's TV series aired on Thames Television 1969-73.
[14] Chief Superintendent.

manager's manual, "Remember, my door is always open." That was reassuring to hear, and I believed him. Months later, when I needed to see him, it was indeed open, but he was obviously surprised I'd taken him up on his offer.

The second in command was a stout, respected and feared former detective who had land in Sicily, where presumably he had Mafia relatives, given the body count of probationers he had dispensed with. He regarded me with a steady suspicion. Gleaming like a polished panel on a patrol car and fresh from training school success, there was nothing he could pin on me. Or so I thought. At the end of the five-minute interview, as I was preparing to leave, he asked, "I assume you call your senior officers sir on sub-division, don't you?" I looked at him quizzically and replied.

"Yes, sir."

"Good," he asserted, "Because you haven't called me it once since you came in here." I suppressed my inner lawyer and decided not to argue that I just had. I would have thought that once every five minutes would have been enough for any man.

The police station in the city centre had been built as part of a large and ambitious civic buildings complex, comprising council offices and chamber, with an adjacent magistrate's court linked via stairs to the central police station cell block.

Completed in 1939, just in time to offer itself for German target practice, the civic centre police station had a classical exterior with a classical lavatorial interior. Shiny white tiles were used in the corridors and cell block area. These tiles were identical to those used in the subterranean public lavatories across the road in Watts Park[15]. I assume they were built at the same time, showing forethought towards the impending Luftwaffe onslaught to come. The contrasting décor in the station building was old dark wood that conveyed the nineteen thirties in its trimming of large round clocks, doors with round brass handles and, of all things, wooden toilet seats.

The men's toilet block was a bleak, poorly lit compartment, containing dark wooden cubicles which had rather faded brown seats atop the white porcelain of the pans. The white cisterns loomed above, like high court judges passing verdicts on your darkest doings. It seemed these were the original seats from 1939 that had been exposed to the varied cheeks of around forty years' worth of

---

[15] Located at Above Bar and Civic Centre Road they are long gone. Pop into the adjacent library toilets instead for a similar architectural experience.

Southampton policing backsides. The faded and eroded varnish was not only a testament to the passage of time but presented a potential health hazard as, although wood imparted a natural warmth, especially on a cold winter's morning, it also possessed a natural absorbency. The best I can say is the seats were well-seasoned. Although I decided to shun usage, the thunderous eruptions, especially post breakfast, of some of the older beat officers suggested they were less fussy or maybe just desperate as there was no viable alternative. There was a senior officer's toilet in the station, but that required a key. I was informed it was still in use years later and that a tube of haemorrhoid cream with an applicator was left lying on the window ledge, presumably for individual and not group use. I'd have expected it to have been left in the constables' lavatories; given that most in that rank were of the view senior officers were, on the whole, a pain in the arse.

On one of my first 2-10 shifts, the section decided on an after-work Indian meal. I was all up for that, and we descended on a small establishment on a hill near a car trader's lot in Bevois Valley called The Manzil. It was opposite a pub that, in those days, sold in the main, very cold lager to bald white men, whose other distinguishing features were the absence of a neck and possibly the possession of a National Front identity card.

    We were in "half blues": shirts with epaulettes removed, uniform trousers and footwear with a "civvie[16] jacket" to make us "incognito". Perhaps we looked like a shift of corporation bus drivers, but somehow, I think not. Most of us wouldn't have been able to fit in the cab.

    As we sat in two rows at a table and were getting stuck into our chicken tikka masalas, a bedraggled drunk with long hair, a long beard, and an even longer overcoat came in and approached the counter, demanding service. His patience threshold was seemingly linked to his level of hunger as he started to berate the poor waiter behind the counter before kicking its fascia somewhat forcibly with heavy workman's boots. A bit of an incident was developing, which I watched from the corner of my eye while my colleagues, all more battle-hardened, off duty and hungry, had their eyes firmly down, focused on their food.

    Unexpectedly, as the drunk embarked on another outburst of vitriol and counter-kicking, a very small Indian man, no more than five feet two in height, came steaming out of the kitchen through short pine swing doors, holding a ladle above his head which was about the same length as him. Screaming some sort of

---

[16] Police speak for your own personal coat.

high-pitched war cry, like an Indian infantryman dispatching an adversary, he proceeded to bring the ladle down with considerable force on the top of the bearded "customer's" head.

The curry creator's intervention certainly cured the kicking. I watched the hungry inebriate place his hand on a visible wound from which blood was now pouring. I again looked around my colleagues, all of whom were still eyes down as if on big night bingo. Eventually, seeing my dutiful concern, which had developed into my standing up, a couple joined me in dusting down Mr Drunk. He was told he was lucky before we showed him the door. I'm not sure we explained in what way his head wound was lucky, but he seemed grateful. The next morning, somewhat concerned by the injury, I checked with the coroner's office, just to be on the safe side.

One night a few months later, I attended a fight in a street nearby in Bedford Place, where an area car driver would tell a man in a white, rapidly reddening T-shirt, who had been glassed on the back of his thick, shaven head, "Don't worry mate, blood spreads; it always looks worse than it is." His crewmate, noted for his empathic treatment of victims, then inspected the injury and cheerfully announced to the shocked man, "Looks like someone's cleaved you a third ear, pal," referring to the flap of bleeding flesh hanging mid-neck. He was at least decent enough not to find a mirror to show the newly aurally enhanced owner. "Couple of stitches mate, and you'll be fine."

Still in my first few weeks, and I was in the pig driven by Cruncher. Stan liked to be in the van a lot, but then they looked very similar, so maybe it was a security/maternal thing. It was around midnight. We were assisting other units with a "domestic dispute": a broad term used to categorise an incident between family members. These can often be very dangerous indeed.

"Domestic" suggests a family argument in a kitchen, perhaps with a sense of something private the police should keep out of. This certainly seemed true at the time of disputes between husbands and wives, where women, overwhelmingly the victims, had scant protection from a police force that didn't deal with minor "common assaults" (those leaving no marks), which were at that time the provenance of the civil courts. In reality, this meant many assaults didn't get dealt with and gave the cops a way out of intervening, leaving the unmatched parties to continue their "dispute". Not all the victims were female; as was the case with one man who showed me a mild graze on his shin, no worse than one inflicted in an under-fives soccer match, which he complained his wife had perpetrated on him. After hearing her side of the story, I was of the view it was a shame she hadn't been able to kick him considerably higher.

In this instance, three brothers were having a "domestic disagreement" on the concrete paving outside of a high-rise block of flats known for being high enough to be capable of performing a " base" parachute jump[17] from (this I know from a confession from a parachuting PC, who, during a particularly boring set of nights, decided to conduct a feasibility study, with, I am glad to report, positive results).

On arrival, the three men were shouting and exchanging punches. We waded in with the other PCs to take hold of them to calm the situation and arrest them for a "Breach of the Peace", a catch-all ancient piece of legislation from, astonishingly, 1361, which was quite useful in these kinds of circumstances.

As I took hold of the right arm of one curly-haired twenty-something sibling, I experienced how an officer could get badly injured in a microsecond. The man, with the force of a first division centre forward, jerked his head around in my direction in what was a highly practised, and presumably often very effective, head-butt manoeuvre. I instinctively blinked and moved back momentarily, and this perhaps was the reason that at the full extension of his neck muscles, his forehead was approximately two millimetres from the end of my nostrils. I then realised I was within one centimetre of having a nose the profile of a hammerhead shark.

It was a sobering experience. Ever since I made it my policy to hold the head of an arrested person who showed signs of violence. This didn't always work out well. Restraining a drunken youth who was angrily head-butting and denting the bonnet of a parked car, I placed my hand behind his head to stop him drawing it back and increasing the force with which he could strike the vehicle. Approaching colleagues told me they thought I was doing a good job of battering his head off the car's engine cover. I can only hope the watching public took a less cynical view, and I am grateful that, at that time, camera phones had not been invented.

During Easter week, I was crewed with an area car driver who was being loaned to Shirley from Portswood for the duration of the night shift, as we were short-staffed. PC Dick Stinting took me to a Chinese takeaway in Shirley Road that, to

---

[17] Parachuting from a fixed point—typically a high structure rather than an aircraft.

remain profitable, understood the need to diversify and accordingly provided fish and chips. As my order was placed on the counter, I put a five-pound note down to pay. Dick, no doubt alarmed that if I paid, he would have to pay, turned to me and said sharply, "Put that away; you don't need to pay in here."

The middle-aged Chinese woman serving glowered with suppressed resentment but said nothing. My tight-fisted colleague was oblivious to her body language. As he stepped out across the threshold that day before Good Friday with his free food, he tripped, and a battered cod skidded across the pavement. Seemingly resurrected, it swam in the rain and muck of the kerbside to be swallowed by a wide-mouthed, hungry drain. Dick looked at me jealously as I tightly clasped my newspaper wrap, but I was as oblivious to his pain as he was to hers. And anyway, mine was haddock.

I don't know why he thought meals were free there. I don't know how often he drove over from his patch to help himself. Another officer had likely told him, after perhaps being given free food himself. When word got around, it could be difficult for a business. Of course, it's completely wrong for the police to accept or expect anything free.

There was certainly in existence a bit of a freebie culture that some officers would exploit. It was explained to me that when police pay was very poor in the sixties and seventies, shopkeepers knew this and tended to look after the local dedicated foot bobby on the beat. Police cars meant a change in this relationship. It didn't occur to a lot of officers that they were just one in a long line abusing an unsustainable practice.

A situation arose where a friendly restaurant manager at the nearby motorway services started providing a cooked breakfast to the early morning motorway traffic patrol crew. Rumour had it she had taken a shine to one officer, but perhaps she just liked the reassuring presence of the police. While one crew a day was acceptable to her (even though it was quite unacceptable within police regulations), ten crews were not. Word had spread, so patrol cars were turning up from all points of the compass. It seems the tipping point came when yet another traffic unit had driven in. What made it intolerable was the badge on the door: it was from another *county*. An officer I worked with, somewhat renowned for being tighter than a whale's arse hole in a deep dive, used to talk about "putting on his buying suit" when shopping. It, of course, was blue.

The city was tense. Rioting in London and Liverpool has spread across the country, and the powers that be didn't want any copycat events in Hampshire. A petrol bomb had been thrown in a local road, not far from The Manzil, by bomber jacket-wearing skinheads who couldn't afford to get their kicks at the football.

The acronym BAME[18] hadn't been invented yet, so the city community area to which it would have been applied was referred to locally as "the jungle". This was, of course, an unfortunate term and desperately inaccurate, as there wasn't an elephant or tiger to be seen anywhere. In their place, on softly lit street corners, were plump prostitutes, parasitic pimps, and a succession of punters in cars, lapping persistently to the general aggravation of residents. The inhabitants themselves, many of whom were Sikh, went about their lives, going to work, visiting the temple, pub, and local supermarket while negotiating the vice that engulfed them.

There was, of course, a policing appreciation at senior level that colloquial terms like "the jungle" were highly inappropriate. To get cops to stop using the term, a new one needed to be fashioned to replace it, and so, slowly, into common usage came the term ICA: Inner City Area. It was a long slog, but it came to be the accepted term over time. Even the locals eventually dropped "the jungle". Now, even the term ICA has long had its day and has been dispensed with after someone had a brainwave and decided to call the area by its actual name, that of Nicholstown-Newtown.

A rapid operation was put in place to ring-fence the ICA with police. As the area was on Central's patch, officers from across the city were deployed, and we were dropped off at strategic points. I found myself seconded in from Shirley, standing with three other officers, one a chirpy bearded local PC, opposite a restaurant called "The Curry Garden". We had been deposited in the correct place.

Our Geordie Chief Superintendent, Mr Shaw, strode towards us, accompanied by a flapping inspector as staff officer. PCs hated being approached by senior officers on the street as protocol demanded they salute, and, not being the army, we generally weren't very good at it. Some bosses got embarrassed by it themselves, and altogether, it was like having to hug a distant auntie in a family where the closest anyone gets is that required to pass the gravy at Christmas. We each awkwardly threw up a weak salute, hoping no one was looking and praying he wouldn't speak to us, as fear of rank switched off brains and simultaneously froze vocal cords. This was the reality of approachable senior managers in the modern police service of 1981.

---

[18] Black, Asian and Minority Ethnic.

The boss was concerned that officers didn't know why they had been deployed. We did, but hadn't been briefed specifically. He asked. At first, no one replied. There was then an overlong silence that was crushingly painful and seemed to confirm the bosses' fears. The local PC, with his helmet set at a jaunty angle and looking like Bluto from the cartoon series Popeye, saved the day by blurting out, "We're here to keep the local yobos out of the jungle, governor." The Boss let the geographical colloquialism wash by in his evident relief that someone knew what the hell they were doing.

And really, that is it. We spent the next few hours in the cold outside St Mary's Fire Station, strictly avoiding the area marked "keep clear". Nothing happened. No one from the station offered a cup of tea, but to be fair, they were probably sleeping or on a day off and, therefore, almost certainly industriously engaged in a second job. (Local word had it that one in ten patios in the city were built by firemen, but I doubt it was more than one in twelve.)

As I stood on the corner with my partner, a small boy emerged from a nearby doorway. He beckoned me to follow him. I entered a small dark room where there was a table and chair. I was invited to sit. He, of course, spoke English as he was born here, but his mum didn't as she wasn't.

The mother placed a bowl of lamb curry in front of me with a small pile of chapattis. It was a very moving moment of appreciation, and I was as grateful for the generosity of spirit as I was genuinely surprised. For a moment, I was at a loss, but then I considered how very frightened they must have been by events. I was further at a loss on a more immediate level—there was no knife or fork. Fortunately, I had the sense to say nothing. Instead, I ate with my fingers using the flatbread. The sauce was rich and spectacularly delicious. I didn't eat anything like it again until a trip to Southall years later. The small boy attended; we talked a little before I bid my farewell, with thanks, to his dignified sari-clad mother. I then stepped outside again to act as protector, replaced by my hungry partner, who didn't know what delectation was in store. Funny how recalling that brings a tear to my eyes: must have been all those spices.

6 Shirley Police Station

The first ten weeks stationed at Shirley flew past as I tried to establish where things were and how to do the multitude of tasks that fell to me. Ensuring there was enough milk for early turn tea was probably my most important job.

Maintaining professional standards of dress was important. Uniformity was regarded as essential; more essential than doing the job well, I often thought. If it was tunics, everyone had to be in a tunic. It was just the same for NATO sweaters. As I looked painfully thin in mine, I didn't like to patrol in it and would try to sneak out the back door in my much smarter and flattering tunic, only to have our pipe-smoking inspector recall me, like an aborted missile, to change. There were stories, told with great pride, of the days of the Southampton City Police, where, if you drove into the city and saw one officer in a greatcoat, every other officer you saw thereafter would be dressed identically. This appealed to those in the service of an obsessive-compulsive disposition, along with supporters of the Chinese communist party, of which there seemed to be many of the former and somewhat fewer of the latter.

One morning in those early weeks, I had just mounted the ground-floor stairs when I was startled by a censorious hissing from my right. "PC Mitchell! Buttons!"

I swung my head around to find myself gazing at the extended sideburns of Inspector Peel, whom I presumed had a genetic connection to the great Sir Robert, given his staunch police-like countenance and zeal for both duty and regulations. I was slightly bewildered by the comment, momentarily thinking about a pantomime before I then frantically started to feel around my tunic's outer pockets and front fasteners until I identified the untethered culprit—the large lower pocket on the right of my tunic. Suitably chastised at letting standards slip, like a Scots guard who has forgotten his sporran, I proceeded on up to the admin department with my papers for typing. I contrast this to the officers of today who wear combat trousers and cycling tops, have crew-cut heads and unshaven faces, making the more rotund among them resemble dirty tennis balls. How times have changed.

Inspector Peel lived for policing. He ran the tightest shift (fortunately not mine) with a rod of iron. No meal breaks of an hour for his shift: regulation forty-five minutes, then out the back door. Anyone loitering around the same door any time before five minutes to booking off time was unceremoniously rebuked and threatened with a deduction for time off. He often patrolled alone and, if on divisional cover, would have three radios on the car seat beside him, each on a different channel for the three subdivisions. He was English: as English as cricket (which he loved) and roast beef. (No vegetarianism here, I suspect. That was the diet of the conquered.) When I wrote a French version of the number seven with a score through the middle to differentiate it from the numeral one, he scowled at me and said with disdain, "What is this?"

"A French number seven, sir," I replied.

He looked at me with a Churchillian gaze. "This is *England*, my boy", he asserted before promptly passing me a bottle of correction fluid.

Any infraction or error, and he let you know about it. Nothing was missed. He was tough but immensely respected as a leader. Quite why you would walk through walls for men like this, I don't know; you just would.

The station at Shirley[19] was a three-story high modern structure of late nineteen sixties vintage with, unsurprisingly, no front-facing windows, just a few high, glass "light bricks" to provide some natural illumination to the parade room. Real windows started on the upper levels out of normal brick-throwing range. The entrance doors were heavy plate glass, set opposite the front enquiry counter, which was staffed twenty-four-seven. The station sat directly on the high street opposite a parade of shops and an ornate Catholic Church[20]. I often wondered whether it was the station, as opposed to the chapel, which obtained the most confessions on a weekly basis.

In those days, before what some in government now might describe as the woke Police and Criminal Evidence Act of 1984, the police could detain people for up to three days in what was known as "local custody". It was not uncommon for a suspect to be arrested on a Friday evening and then be left over the weekend before an interview the following Monday. Then, lawyers in police stations were as rare as constables on the beat are now. Although Shirley Station's three cells were modern and light, they were also desolate and bleak. Little wonder that (a) confessions tended to follow after what amounted to three days of solitary confinement and (b) the law was changed, and for the better, with a starting point of twenty-four hours maximum detention without charge. Oh, how some officers moaned about the shorter time frame and the need to go out and collect evidence.

---

[19] Located in a perfect High Street location for public accessibility and reassurance, the police were relegated onto an industrial estate beside a motorway and replaced by a supermarket.
[20] Located in a perfect High Street location for public accessibility and reassurance, it is still in situ.

There were several peculiarities I encountered in this modern and quite pleasant police station. Traffic accident forms were A4 in length but half the standard width. The reason: they were designed to fit the narrow drawers at HQ traffic administration.

The report writing room itself was small and cosy and had three booths with a telephone in each. This was very handy for one of the beat officers, who used to be entertained by his Essex-based girlfriend for hours with conversations for which, these days, people pay good money. You'd be surprised how many officers could fit in there at a push.

Behind the front office counter were various files. There was a bail reporting book where persons on bail from court were obliged to come in and "sign on" in an effort to constrain them from absconding. For what good purpose, I don't know: none of them had the bus fare to skip to Bournemouth, let alone Buenos Aires.

Every call to the police generated a "G4 in message". Each one had to be completed with a result and filed by a sergeant who tore the corner off to show it had been finished. I was told of a *very* large force where one station had a bit of an honesty and integrity "problem" south of the river in the 1970s. Officers were so brazen and discipline so lax that some messages were allegedly endorsed "dealing and stealing". Hard to believe, I know.

Behind the front counter was the controller's booth, where non-urgent calls were received and units dispatched. Usually, much older shift members fulfilled the role as it was sedentary, warm, close to a toilet, and most youngsters preferred being out. One controller would come in his cardigan and slippers. Many of the controllers were officers who had served in the Southampton city force from before the 1967 amalgamations. They had all worked foot beats in a system of policing long gone by 1981. They knew every back alley and the location of every tea stop going.

Adjacent to the controller was a receptionist who monitored the switchboard and dealt with sending and receiving telex messages. The latter had to be sent to notify the Force Intelligence Bureau (FIB) of property stolen in a burglary, a stolen car or a missing person. The fragrant receptionist's area was always popular, especially with divorced and separated male officers, and was where shift tea breaks occurred.

The radio room housed personal radios and some very long, yellow baseball bats fashioned like super-sized truncheons. These were for a specific purpose. There was a drug warehouse on the patch. It was alarmed with a link to the station. It was reasoned that if it were burgled, it would be by a criminal gang, which would almost certainly be armed. In this case, it was judged only sensible that the police were able to deal with this threat by the use of these massive yellow truncheons, designed, presumably, to bat the bullets away.

There was a safe and a separate crime property store, for which the station sergeant kept the keys. On the first floor lurked the CID offices and the office of the Special Branch. The SB office was different as it had a Yale lock, and the officers working there were the only ones with access. They generally dressed like Moss Bros tailors' dummies and tended to engage in conversation about as much as well.

The chief inspector in charge of the subdivision was on this floor along with the admin manager, typists, and crime prevention officer. The latter was so important that it had a whole person (non-police officer) dedicated to it.

The top floor contained the recreational area. There was a huge unused industrial kitchen with a large dance floor area and bar with seating. Also available was a pool table that got plenty of use on nights (during meal breaks) and, of course, the obligatory fruit machine that certain officers just couldn't leave alone. The bar was open certain days of the week and was often used after late turns, where the duty detective constable could often be found gathering local intelligence from the barmaid.

This design of the station was from a different age. Many forces didn't have bars in police stations due to the obvious conflict around drink driving and stations needing to be licensed premises. Instead, they had bespoke social clubs. As time progressed, bars closed, but this was 1981, and Shirley's bar was open, and every so often, there would be a heavily attended disco with the station windows thrown open due to the heat. Of course, this meant a steady flow of indignant calls complaining about police partying. Not a particularly good advertisement. No one really wants to hear Slade's greatest hits at any time. Still, with bar prices low and fun social functions, there was a much lighter mood than at the official Southampton Police Club. I'm not quite sure what the weekend occupants of the cells two floors down below thought, though.

The sergeant at Shirley responsible for probationary constables sourced my initial accommodation in a backwater street on the edges of Millbrook. My landlady was a sprightly widow whose husband had passed away shortly after retirement at the age of sixty-five, a fate that seemed to be experienced by a lot of male manual labourers at that time.

I occupied the bedroom at the back of the house. It had depressingly dark wood furniture where I would sleep until five p.m. on "nights" until I felt my life slipping away, and I forced myself to get up earlier. I never really felt comfortable in the digs and never took my clothes out of my trusty green suitcase to place them in the drawers. I wasn't staying.

The landlady had hoped for some company of an evening, but sitting in front of a television was not my idea of a good time, and I had a particular disdain for adverts.

Because I spent periods at my family home on days off, I parsimoniously sought to renegotiate the weekly rate. She agreed reluctantly, but then retaliated by dropping the processed meat from my sandwiches. I became an involuntary vegetarian. The final blow to our edgy relationship occurred when I blotted my copybook by making the unforgivable error of forgetting to watch her and her kin compete in a television show called "Family Fortunes." It was a big-money game show hosted by comedic quizmaster Bob Monkhouse. Alas, no family fortune was to be won as they failed to answer any questions at all, struggling indeed with the easier ones designed to establish identity, despite Uncle Bob's encouragement. There was no catch-up TV in those days, so if you missed it, you missed it, and I missed it. It was probably fortuitous that, after just a few months, I moved out, as shortly after, I encountered her affable adult son at the rear of the station, standing beside a WPC. I looked at him quizzically as I opened the plate-glass rear door. "Hello, what are you doing here?"

"I've done a stupid thing. Shoplifting."

He had decided to unlawfully appropriate an electric drill from B&Q (well, they were expensive), but hadn't factored in the use of store detectives. I felt sorry for him in his embarrassment, while being disappointed with him at the same time. I suspected he felt pretty much the same.

There had been one glowing benefit to those digs: they were located in the sub-division. One ferociously cold night, when the snow blew with a near-Alaskan frenzy, I was able to sneak home to warm up in the kitchen for a few minutes as a break from the pointless marching about in a blizzard as though I was the ghost of a delirious Captain Scott.

There was very little necessity for foot patrols at night after the pubs had shut, but they were a throwback to a different age of policing and the role of night watchman. There was certainly absolutely no point in walking the beat in torrential rain or heavy snow. This, though, was seen as a task that somehow endowed masculinity, like not washing your hands after peeing or spitting chewing gum into a station urinal.

Shortly after the Family Fortunes fiasco, a vacancy occurred at the Southampton police hostel. Like a bandit who'd just blagged a big city bank, I grabbed my already packed suitcase and rapidly hot-footed it a mile or so east to the city centre and a friendly world that once again offered the delights of processed meats.

There were three dog cells corresponding to the three adult cells at Shirley. The downside for the dogs was their accommodation was outside and cold. Their compensation, however, was that the food was better. For probationers, the upside of the adult cells was there was a station cleaner. The downside to the dog pound for junior probationers was, cleaning was up to them, with all the glamour that entailed, and which, for some inexplicable reason, you never saw on Z Cars. I never once saw Bert Lynch trying to tease a terrier's turd into a bin bag or dispose of a Doberman's dump. It wasn't in that Met recruiting film, either.

One probationer, whose attendance on time for an early turn was entirely dependent on whether he managed to hitch a lift to work from his home twenty-five miles away, was given dog doo-doo duty one Wednesday morning. To hose the offending pen, he decided to attach the poo-producing pooch to a metal "Police Accident" sign (usually deployed as a warning at traffic accidents) rather than take the more conventional and safer route of relocating the animal in one of the other two dog detention dens.

The sign, although sufficient to resist a strong wind, was not exactly a permanent anchor. With his jailer in the dark recesses of the pound, attending to the animal's still warm bodily excretions, the retriever, whose name should have been Ronnie, decided to make a break for it and, with a woof, legged it, times four, out the Brigg and rear yard, dragging the clanging sign behind it.

Nicknamed Wingnut, either for his protruding ears or due to the judgment he had a screw loose, the constable, seeing the escape, failed to differentiate between human and canine detention and immediately called for a posse as he legged it down the high street at full pelt, truncheon drawn, in pursuit of the sloppy tongued hound that was enjoying the chase of a lifetime; dragging the very visible and noisy sign behind it. Quite what the astonished shoppers thought, particularly about the truncheon, I don't know. Luckily, he never caught the fleeing felon, so we were spared the complaints that battering it senseless would have inevitably generated. Those in high places in the station did not see his actions as a good example of decision-making, and, aggregated with other transgressions, the probationer found himself exiting the service for a life less intellectually demanding, and I believe, promptly joined the prison service.

Each animal cage was firmly built in grey mesh and steel with a small gap between the floor and partition. A large, dark, and handsome mastiff-type animal was later sequestered in the middle cell. He was an unhappy dog with a short temper, and we christened him Heathcliff. He had been found wandering on waste ground and hauled, snarling, into the station by a do-gooding RSPCA type. Dogs tended to stay three days awaiting a claimant; thereafter, they were shipped out to their "final destination".

A few hours later, a rather cute, playful, amber-coloured lost pup arrived. The duty desk officer assured those depositing that it would be safe and well looked after before promptly incarcerating the dog child in pen number one. Well, we couldn't really have it running around the station, although that might have happened in more rural parts, where various animals, domestic and wild, could occasionally be found inhabiting parts of the premises: a partridge in the post box, a rabbit in the radio room, a dead deer hanging in an outhouse like an Italian dictator, that sort of thing.

The station duty officer went for a meal break, and Sue took over. As kindly a soul as you could imagine, nothing warmed her heart more than babies and puppies, so it was with great pleasure that she led the young couple who owned the pup out into the backyard to reclaim their nearest and dearest, who had it seemed, escaped through a negligently unfastened cat flap.

Smiles of warm delight at the reuniting were replaced with shrieks of horror that emanated after the pound door was opened, as, although the entire pup was present, it was apparent that a preliminary form of reuniting was going to be called for: namely, the re-unification of its head to its body.

It transpired that Heathcliff had not projected the face of his beloved Cathy onto the unfortunate mite that had pushed its friendly, innocently naive head under the metal guard rail sitting three inches off the concrete floor. Instead, in an act of wanton violence, Heathcliff had severed the pup's neck with a momentary flexing of his powerful jaws. The tear-stricken owners left empty-handed, while I was dispatched to find tissues for Sue and a brown paper sack for body recovery.

"Look on the bright side, Brian," joked Rick Radweldt, the senior probationer on the shift. "At least it didn't have time to shit all over the floor."

No, Rick, it didn't. But that murdering bastard Heathcliff did.

The conflicts of having a bar in a police station were highlighted one evening when our benign shift inspector was departing for a last posting before heading for retirement. The shift had come in on a day off for a 7.30 p.m. start, with a late evening planned for some (me).

The patrol sergeant assumed the responsibility of saying a few awkward words: the precursor to handing over the obligatory card and pewter tankard. Also in the bar were a couple of WPCs from another shift who were also on a night out. One, well known for her incendiary disposition, was wearing a white cotton dress that, due to her sitting in a car against a PVC seat, had a very noticeable concertina column of creases up the back. A question as to whether she kept her clothes in a matchbox rather than a wardrobe was not met with the mirth expected, and she exploded off her barstool with indignation. This added to a slightly edgy atmosphere that was additionally fueled by a few detectives who had been there since five, one being none other than the detective inspector.

Normally a serious, dignified, if brusque individual, DI Cash had been on the lash. He was tieless and open-necked, which, compared to his normal attire, was akin to nakedness. As our sergeant lamented the departure of the shift leader with a surfeit of insincerity, Cash expressed the broadly collective view more authentically: he erupted in a guffaw that was simultaneously slightly amusing and very embarrassing. Some dark looks were rightly shot at the detective, who further interrupted proceedings by declaring, "Anyone here wants trouble? If you want trouble, I'll give you trouble; I was a para." (There was no elaboration made, despite a later suggestion by a DC, that his exact posting had been in the catering corps.) The challenge to fight ignored, there was a gentle ripple of applause followed by an awkward handing over of the receptacle that would probably never be filled with anything other than dust.

After further drinking, a decision was made to attend The Magnum Club: on the basis it was actually open. One of the older DCs knew the management, and it seemed we would be well received. This was now a CID operation. The club was well known in the city as being an alternative venue with a mainly gay and transgender clientele. A small group attended, led by Cash, accompanied by his DCs, the WPCs (who were effervescent after their white wine spritzers), me, and a long, thin, especially upright, if not uptight, young Scot called Cameron, who was a civilian police employee and member of the force band. (He had played a wind instrument alongside the departing inspector.)

As we entered the pitifully empty, darkly smoky and tired-looking club, we noticed a cigarette machine where the money went in the top, and the cigarettes were dispensed at the bottom. It was situated behind a counter, so you had to bend over to get them. The two leering doormen considered this a very funny joke for a gay club, and I smiled with them while feeling thankful that I didn't smoke. I stood with a pint of lager, watching a few game dancers as Cash continued his belligerent behaviour, although in a more moderate form. Cameron was feeling uncomfortable, it seemed. Standing beside me, like a cross between an emaciated caber and a sentry, he uttered matter-of-factly, "I'd rather piss myself than go to the bogs in here."

His reserve was somewhat over-the-top, but he was clearly well out of his comfort zone, like an Englishman at a Burns night supper. This, of course, was 1981. Times were changing, and the city had an alternative scene, but we were a long way from LGBTQ+, and we were at the threshold of the awful AIDS outbreak of the 1980s. We watched as a few couples danced. Then Cameron, who'd had a few before we arrived, said, "I need to go to the bog. Come with me so we can watch each other's arses."

I'm not quite sure he got the irony, but as I needed to go, I followed him, much to the interest of the doormen. I re-joined our group and engaged in job talk and discussions with the club manager. It occurred to me that membership of a club like this was liable to get you thrown out of training school. At least we were there. Progress of sorts? Well, that was how it was then.

7 Brewery Trip

The weather was getting warmer, and people were getting thirsty. The shift's social luminaries decided it was time to go on a brewery trip.

Team spirit is essential in any line of work, but more so in jobs where you rely on your colleagues watching your back. Decompression from the cumulative demands of conflict, the harshness of police work, and the four-shift system is important. Assaults, sudden deaths, child abuse, injury traffic accidents, all take their toll. It's not just girls who want to have fun, as Cyndi Lauper was to tell us shortly after.

OK. There rests the case for the defence for what was to follow.

There being a close social bond between our shift at Shirley and the corresponding shift at Central, it was decided there would be a combined outing to a provincial brewery in another county to the west. A luxury coach was hired at an advantageous rate by social secretary Cruncher through a contact at a local travel company. Later, this contact would prove more helpful than we could ever imagine.

Although the mechanics of beer making had no more interest to me than the mechanics of my car, I appreciated that this might be a pleasant day away and an opportunity to bond with new colleagues. I'd also never been on a visit to a brewery. Interestingly, I've never been inclined to go on one since.

There was a bit of a three-line whip, with the affably sociable central inspector, Delbert Tart, the senior officer present. Alongside him was the steward of the police club, an elfin-looking man called Len Gale, who always dressed immaculately. A censorious Welsh sergeant, Phil Rill, accompanied these two dignitaries along with a large number of boisterous boys in and out of blue. Of the women on shift, all but one on this occasion had made the insightful decision not to attend. I was quite pleased as the coach was passing near my hometown, where I tended to stay on my days off.

About the appointed hour, I was standing in the bar of what was The Ferndown Hotel, a large, darkly wooded and imposing building, with just a young woman behind the bar for company. It was midday, and she was busy doing nothing. I suggested she get prepared for a surge in business by a factor of fifty. She laughed and asked why. I replied that in about five minutes, fifty thirsty blokes were going to walk through the door demanding a pint. Well, fifty pints. She giggled again and smiled indolently. The cavernous bar was as empty and quiet as a Methodist church on a Monday. This, however, being a Wednesday, meant the serenity was temporary. Pretty much on time, Delbert and the entire entourage from the coach poured in. The usual joke about it being my round was made, and, in response, I bought myself a pint. The pub sold beer from the vats we were visiting, so everyone got a taste of what was to come, beer-wise anyway.

After refreshments, we moved off to a charming county town and its elegant Victorian brewery, where we were offered the normal or short tour. The first implies some level of genuine interest in, or at least respect for, the premises and its history. The second is basically a shortcut from the brew kettle straight to the bar, and it was the second that was overwhelmingly voted for by the cultured crew. To be fair, it transpired many of the entourage had been on several trips like this before and so found the prospect of a full tour as dull as the contents of a ditch in Dagenham, even if the product wasn't.

We strolled past a few bags of finings and looked into a large receptacle that looked like a sewage treatment plant. A few of the party sniggered like schoolboys, with the inevitable jokes about falling in being a good way to die. We were then shown to the bar. This was a large but windowless room in the bowels of the building. Here you could drink for free for the next hour using half-pint glasses. The idea for some was to drink as much as they could in the time allowed. It was essentially a kind of drinker's bar billiards.

Given the generosity and hospitality provided, the brewery management hoped we would consume their beer in the future. This, of course, was dependent on whether or not they supplied to the area where we mostly lived, and in this case, they didn't. It's a shame because it was pretty good beer. Some forward-thinking individuals had brought along five-litre containers to fill from the pumps for home, presumably to make up for the absence of the brew in their local pub. Two of the group helpfully assisted the young woman behind the bar by joining her to speed up the process, essentially relieving her of her duties.

Some breweries restrict free pints to one or two to reduce drunkenness and control expenditure. Many now charge for the experience. In this golden time of free compressed air on garage forecourts, breweries could be rather too relaxed and get exploited by seasoned drinkers, who could drain reserves like a herd of elephants at a watering hole in a drought.

Naturally, its strongest ale, oddly named "Mangleshoot"—presumably in homage to some member of the local landed gentry with a keen talent for shooting peasants (sorry, pheasants)—was in greatest demand, with the barrel needing changing more than once. There was an expansive table of cheese and salad sandwiches, which were demolished like a mill chimney in Chorley: quickly and with plenty of mess.

As the beer flowed, the thirstier and less restrained members of the congregation became increasingly raucous, rather like a football crowd then or a cricket crowd now. There was a bit of play-fighting and a general letting down of hair (as far as short back and sides allowed).

The one woman on the excursion found she had a small problem. She needed to use the facilities, but, of course, there wasn't a woman's toilet in what was then an exclusively male domain. The management, sensitively understanding her predicament, graciously gave her the key to their rather splendidly appointed executive lavatory. Alas, her intentions didn't quite marry up with their expectations, as she had overindulged to the point that she needed to be sick, and this she did with unerring inaccuracy, exploding like a lawn sprinkler at high pressure. The only good news was that the walls were already painted in a fetching shade of matt orange.

The brewery management, fearing the month's profit margin was in jeopardy, gently called proceedings to a close, and the band of beer-bloated brothers (and less bloated sister) emptied out of the bar into the daylight, lugging containers of ale, like pirates hauling barrels of brandy to a long boat on an abandoned beach.

The thinly moustached coach driver was large, discreet, and quietly resigned to his task. He was now under no illusion that he had a mission: get the group home and the coach back to the depot unscathed. Given there was a no-drink or food policy on board, he was in for a hard time.

We were barely at the town limits and ten minutes into the return journey when several of the congregation decided they needed a toilet stop. There was a small car park with a grey prefabricated public convenience off the main road, mainly used by families heading for holidays in the West Country.

By this time, the considerably merry Inspector Tart, a gentle, kindly man, more loved perhaps than respected, had removed his dental plate and was grinning vacuously, exposing the black gaps where his plastic canine teeth had been.

Phil Rill, a usually serious individual with an eye on promotion and a keen compulsion to enforce hat-wearing on duty, had become a dilated-eyed loon, who, as we climbed down from the bus, grabbed the untethered teeth and promptly ran over to a car packed with suitcases, holiday effects, and a family of four eating sandwiches. Rill proceeded to prostrate himself on the bonnet of the car, shoving the slightly soiled dental plate in front of the feeding family while giggling like the five-year-old he had become. The children responded in kind; the adults similarly, but with wary looks, casting glances to the side as if scouting for a mental health search party.

Excitedly, Rill then ran to other cars to repeat his performance as a line of impatient men queued in and out of the gentlemen's toilet. The more sober in the group rounded up the stragglers, and as the coach pulled away, Tart was reunited with his teeth. This proved to almost be a mistake because he was soon close to losing them again. Feeling ill with the movement of the bus, Tart struggled the short distance to the front and induced the driver to open the coach door while in motion so that the mixture churning in his stomach could be liberated. The driver, apprehending the potential dangers both to upholstery and the inspector, slowed down to let Delbert stick his head out the door, held by his belt by a more sober and health and safety conscious Stan. Unfortunately, the wind was against Delbert and the coach: the majority of the vomit blew back across the subdued cream hues of his shirt, jacket, and tie in a modernist artistic style, redolent of Jackson Pollock, simultaneously pebble dashing the length of the moving bus. Fortunately, this proved nothing significant: only requiring the coach company to have it professionally steam cleaned.

Proceedings, though, were not at an end. The most boisterous and mischievous were, where they always are on a school trip: at the back of the bus.

Someone there had the idea of piggyback fighting, and so three pairs were trying to gallop like jousters up and down the coach aisle to around the seats at the halfway point. From here forward, the more sensible and sober were sitting, trying to pretend that what was going on behind them wasn't happening, or if it was, it was nothing to do with them.

I was sitting at the cusp of the two groups, to the right, in the aisle seat. A glance up over my left shoulder, and I could see a battle between two pairs with a combined weight of sixty stone. To my left was Len, the small and anxious steward of the police club, a professional in the licensing business, and a gentleman who was demonstrably very unhappy at events and was considerably less happy when two of the combatants fell across his lap. The rider in this rather brutish and ugly coupling struck the huge plate-glass window. Designed to withstand many things, being struck by a force of approximately thirty stone wasn't one of them, and the window popped out in its entirety. In a second, a five-foot-wide sheet of glass shattered explosively on the pavement of the village we were passing through.

I jumped forward and grabbed hold of the Rough Rider, whose head and upper body were protruding, like a Red Setter on a family outing, through the gaping hole. My actions needed to be quick: I had seen a metal plate on a pole just seconds away and pulled him back through just before he had "Request Stop" indelibly imprinted into his forehead.

The bus halted, and Stan climbed out with the dumbstruck driver and Phil Rill. Del wanted to join them as senior officer on watch, but the few bus steps down were a bit much for him, and he dropped back into his seat in a state of mild confusion, events passing at a rate beyond his ability to process them. The bus had gone very quiet as the impact of events sank into befuddled heads. After a few moments, Phil Rill climbed back aboard the bus to address the hushed and shocked congregation. I resisted the urge to introduce him with, "Here's Johnny!"

The former traffic sergeant swayed slightly, trying to keep a grasp of his rational faculties. He then relayed the only news he thought important, given there was no human being lying among the shattered pieces of glass. "Right, it's alright, it's alright, no need to worry, lads. This is not a reportable accident."

And we didn't even have to exchange names and addresses.

The trip home was considerably more subdued but windier, which at least helpfully vented the open space of the acidic odour from Delbert's clothes.

By the good fortune of getting picked up last, I got off first and waved the bus goodbye meekly, after an awkward thanks to the driver. I watched as it pulled away like a galleon limping back to port after a bruising battle with the Spanish Armada.

The story got out, and the press called the coach company. But this was 1981, and they were loyally tight-lipped. God bless them.

8 No Dignity in Dying

My encounters with death so far in life had been few and remote. A grandparent a decade before whom I barely knew, as he lived in another country. A sixteen-year-old boy, just out of school, crushed to death by a forklift truck. I hardly knew him, but his death profoundly affected friends of mine. Another boy who had left our school for London, a talented runner, was killed in a motorcycle accident along with his girlfriend.

These events signposted that death was around. They were discomforting and disturbing, but weren't at the forefront of my mind. There's a curiosity, a fascination the young have with something they feel is far away and for others, not for them.

In police culture, dealing with a death was a rite of passage to be negotiated. Would you crack and prove yourself emotionally incapable of doing the job? Recruits talked about it, and members of your shift waited until the fateful time the radio selected you for your first "G28". It's interesting how the number of the form used to record a death became the term used to describe it, as though, from the start, emotional distance was being inserted between officer and subject. I recall receiving the message for my first. I was sitting, taking details in the parade room with all eyes fixed firmly on me.

All probationers are asked the same question by colleagues, "Have you ever seen a dead body?" It's almost always the case that they haven't. In days gone by, young officers were taken along to post-mortems, the pretext being that the ability to withstand this was part of the job (it wasn't: only senior detectives investigating suspicious deaths need to be present). To show disgust, feel sick, or faint would be immediately relayed back to colleagues, and your respect in the workplace forever damaged. If you fainted, you'd be hard-pressed to live it down. By 1981, the requirement, as part of training, to attend a PM had been dropped.

There was a focus on emotional hardness and physical capability (to be handy in a fight was highly esteemed). These were very traditionally male characteristics from a very male-dominated workplace. The same characteristics were seen in the military and other industries.

I had read the autobiography of the former Metropolitan Police Commissioner, Sir Robert Mark[21]. In it, he mentions his early days as a young constable in Manchester and how, when bodies were removed down the stairs of tenements, it was the probationary constable who was at the bottom end and, as a consequence, found himself doused in whatever liberated bodily fluids had worked their way out of the cadaver. It apparently amused the hell out of senior PCs.

There were several deaths I experienced during those early months of police service, and no matter how blasé I might have appeared or how seemingly detached I might have been, each event created an enduring image as I remember the impact on me and on those who were close to the deceased.

In my early days on shift, I was fortunate to work with a crafty and insightful officer who stood in for my tutor constable on some occasions when she was away. PC Nick Frost insisted I wear a coat in the patrol car and have the window down because I would be less inclined to get out if sitting in shirt sleeves, with the heater on full blast, on a wet winter's night. He was right.

He also told me that plenty of people didn't like the police, and dealing with a sudden death was a time we could "make friends". He said that how the police

---

[21]] In the Office of Constable Sir Robert Mark 1978.

dealt with the departed and their loved ones would remain with those individuals for the duration of their lives and shape their attitudes toward the service. It was insightful and touching and a rare, empathic lesson from an officer who was a bit different from the rest.

The first death I attended was of a well-built, emphysemic manual labourer. Peacefully lying in bed, covers pulled up, his waxy face was the colour of parchment. His tearful relatives sat on the opposite side of the mattress. He was disconcertingly young at just fifty-three. It was a straightforward and gentle introduction.

Less straightforward was the next. On a Sunday afternoon, straight from parading for duty—an old-fashioned term as we were always sat down—I was told to attend a death at Southampton General Hospital (SGH). I was driven there by a disinterested and lethargic colleague who understood I'd be doing the work, and he wouldn't.

I found myself in an ambulance parked outside accident and emergency. The man, who was about 70, lived in a street of terraced houses near the hospital. This proximity did not save him. As he had been pronounced dead in the ambulance, he hadn't been moved into the hospital or its mortuary. Instead, he was to be taken to the city mortuary a few miles away.

My initial job was to check the body for injuries and secure any property. To check the body properly for injuries or foul play would involve pretty much stripping it, which, in most cases, was completely impractical, so my examination was fairly cursory, given the story from the ambulance crew, and involved looking for the more obvious signs of crime, like knives protruding at right angles from the chest cavity and so on. Unsurprisingly, I didn't find any, despite the old joke that the quickest way to a man's heart is through his chest.

Really, I was looking for any items of value in his pockets. At this point, I learned a similar lesson to that visited upon Sir Robert Mark and found that, not unsurprisingly, his left trouser pocket was wet. Another lesson for the future: wear gloves, Brian.

I removed keys and some change with a distasteful expression. I noted the relevant times from the ambulance staff (those of arrival and confirmation of death by a doctor), and then we drove round to his home, where I spoke to the only person present, his sexagenarian wife.

After asking her gently if I could wash my hands, I accepted the offer of a mug of tea, but for a reason connected to a heightened awareness regarding cleanliness, I couldn't bring myself to drink it. I realised her offer of tea, polite, of course, served to give her a buffer between my arrival and having to deal with the business at hand. I talked to the lady who told me her husband had sat opposite her as they watched television and said, "I'm going now," and promptly did. I found this insight both fascinating and profoundly unsettling. What had caused his momentary awareness of his immediate demise?

Some questions needed to be asked, and I had the official form that posed them. The obvious ones are the full details of the deceased, where born, next of kin, and then a question relating to whether there will be a cremation or burial. This is often a disconcerting question for shocked relatives, and it feels too soon and insensitive to be asking it. However, it is on the form and, therefore, always asked, as the coroner's office wants to know. (I was told this was in case the death was suspicious. You can't exhume a cremated cadaver.)

There is a section on the G28 to collect information about the deceased's activities in the previous 24 hours, including details of what they last ate. This, presumably, is for the pathologist to tally up the sausage, egg, and chips against any remnants of ground glass or any other suspicious substance. It's a question that usually flummoxes relatives, who immediately worry that they may have inadvertently poisoned their loved one or, given the condemned man is supposed to have eaten a last hearty meal, they might feel guilty at the paucity of the final offering they had provided. Suddenly, a pork pie and piccalilli doesn't seem quite so fitting.

I gave her the few pieces of property I recovered from her husband. She then dropped the bombshell, "What about his wallet?"

"What wallet?" I responded, remembering the admonition from training school of the three things most likely to get an officer in trouble: property, money, and women.

"The wallet he had in his back pocket," she retorted in a concerned tone.

That would be the back pocket he was lying on in the ambulance, which I didn't search then.

I told her I would deal with this and be back. I explained the predicament to my driver, and we nipped back around to A&E to discover the system had been remarkably efficient for a Sunday. The body had already been removed to the city mortuary, which was at Town Quay on central sub-division. My anxiety was rising as we were now in a game of "find the cash", and it occurred to me, darkly, that this could be a new TV quest show format. Someone was reading my mind, as Anneke Rice popped up shortly afterwards with" Treasure Hunt". It also occurred to me that the cash in his wallet might be *their only cash,* given the modesty of their living conditions.

The mortuary was closed, of course, this being the weekend, so we had to drive to the city centre police station, where a spare key was kept on a hook in the station sergeant's office. The key was a standard front door size, but to ensure it was not lost, it was attached to a piece of wood the size of a portable television. It could reasonably have had use as a life raft.

I hauled the key and its attachment down to the discrete and dreary premises near the docks. It and the area were deserted. We entered the clinical, bleached building. It was, of course, a dormitory of death and concomitantly silent.

In the main examination room were stainless steel tables slightly angled towards a drain. The place was immaculately clean, which was not the case a few months later when I brought a family member to a viewing of a deceased relative in the small chapel attached to the building. Getting no reply from ringing the front doorbell, I sauntered through the side gate with the middle-aged lady in tow to be met by a frantic mortuary assistant, distinctive in a translucent green plastic apron on which I could see rivulets of blood trickling towards the floor. He was desperately signalling to me through the full-length glass side door to reverse and return to the front of the building. Shocked at the sight of him, the penny dropped, and I rapidly rounded on the lady, obscuring her view and distracting her attention with a huge smile and arms thrown wide as I shepherded her away from the grim business end of proceedings. Another on-the-job lesson learned.

On this Sunday, we were alone, and our task was fairly straightforward: find the body. Fortunately, as I'd seen him in the last two hours, this was less difficult than it might have been. I pulled open the heavy steel doors that lined the refrigerated wall and slid out the shelves on runners to find our deceased. Mortuary fridges do not discriminate. They contain the spectrum of local humanity. They are sad, sobering, humbling, and brutal.

Having found my man, I was relieved and, this time wearing gloves, I recovered every item of value, including his fat wallet, and replaced him respectfully and carefully. A colleague on a similar mission had a less fortunate experience. Pulling on the draw too forcefully, it shot out on its smooth, well-oiled runners, the body lurching onto the floor and, in the process, rendering a post-mortem wound to the skull. Aghast that the pathologist might suspect a murder on the next morning's examination, he had to submit a rapid report explaining the unfortunate mishap and the reason he'd been in the mortuary at midnight in the first place.

On returning to the widow, the situation had changed at her home. As I stepped from the hallway into the small living room, I was met with a cacophony from the forty or so people squatting on the floor around the lady, who was sitting prominently, like royalty, on a dining chair towards the back and centre of the room. A coronation of sorts seemed to be in progress.

On my entry, the noise ceased abruptly. There was silence, and eighty eyes were upon me as the family tribe watched my every move. This was an area where not only did everyone know everyone, but everyone was related to everyone, and every immediate relative had quickly assembled to support the widow and pay respects.

I picked my way gingerly, barely finding the space to lay down a boot between the packed bodies that lay between me and her. I returned the property against a signature and conveyed my condolences for her loss under the intense pressure of the gazing mass of relatives who looked on as though watching some ritual in which I dare not make a mistake.

The business done, I respectfully tiptoed out. This triggered the silence to break, and the room detonated in a hubbub of excited conversation. I returned to the station to complete the paperwork and fax the G28 form through to the coroner's officer for the morning. Before I did this, the patrol sergeant checked it and asked, "What do you mean there are no entries?"

"I thought you said check for any entries?"

"I said injuries!"

Oh well, not much difference except the pathologist might have been puzzled at my declaring I had found a mouth, nostrils, and an arse hole.

About 10.30 p.m. on a quiet, wet Tuesday night, the area car got a call to a mock Tudor pub in a residential street near the docks. A sudden death had been reported. We pulled onto an empty forecourt and walked in from the drizzle. The room was long, narrow, and devoid of much comfort or any warmth.

The barman was drying a glass behind the counter. A dead man was lying on his back on the floor in front of the bar, with two other men sitting at a small table adjacent, with small dotted tiles between them. The two men didn't know him, but as they'd only recently bought their drinks, they seemed determined to finish what they'd started and didn't feel the need to move. On the bar, separating the barman and the prone recently departed customer, was a glass of frothy and lively bitter, with no more than a half-inch missing.

"If you're offering a drink, I'm happy for anything except what he's just had," my partner observed, trying to raise the mood with a dose of gallows police humour that was famous for its sledgehammer insensitivity but also helped to shield the utterer from the vicissitudes of life. It was clear no one was in the mood for laughing.

The edge taken off their night; more it seemed by the arrival of the police than the cadaver by the counter, the two players slowly packed away their dominoes, downed their pints and left. I obtained what details I could from the barman, who witnessed the man's collapse just a short while before.

The dead man looked old. His face was battered, with thread-like red veins crisscrossing his cheeks. He was wearing a black reefer jacket. We made enquiries and found he had been staying just a few hundred yards away in a guest house. He had a National Union of Seamen membership card that denoted an age of just fifty-four. I would have put him at almost 20 years older than that. I ruminated about the harshness of his life working as a merchant seaman with no fixed home, getting work aboard ship where he could, staying in down-at-heel guesthouses when he couldn't, drinking in dockside pubs, and expiring on a wet Tuesday night beside strangers and a box of dominoes, his last act to sip on a pint of beer. Here was a man whose life could've been taken straight out of Orwell's "The Road to Wigan Pier". I remember feeling sad thinking about the cold, damp, lonely harshness of this end. What stories could this man have told? I hoped he didn't always drink alone. Of course, he didn't.

On another occasion, a dead man spoke to me, and no, it wasn't just after I'd been abducted by aliens. The man had expired on a sofa in the front room of his small, terraced house in Freemantle after a bout of drinking.

As I took hold of his arms to pull him into an upright position (to check for injuries, not entries), he made a low, sustained "ah" sound, like when a doctor asks you to "say ah" when inspecting your tonsils. This spontaneous sound was less surprising to me than the adjacent, previously cheery relative who had thought she was about to inherit the house. She jumped like a mouse that's just realised it's stepped onto a spring-loaded piece of cheese.

The action of pulling the man into an upright position forced the air out of his lungs, vibrating his vocal cords and creating the sound. Fortunately, I had been alerted to the possibility of this occurring at training school and was surprisingly unfazed. The relative regained both her colour and cheer on the news that he was, in fact, still very dead.

It has been my abiding view that death is seldom dignified, and if it is, it is usually by luck. There is a very clinical, matter-of-fact industry that sits behind it. Many people play a part: the police are but one group. Maybe it's due to my experiences, but it has always seemed odd to me that the vast majority of us will have to go through the hideously barbaric indignity of a public post-mortem when, in other countries, this is not always the norm. Even where it is, there are non-invasive alternatives.[22] Unfortunately, some profit from butchery. I never met a poor pathologist.

Later in my probation, when I could drive police cars, I found myself returning property to a bereaved woman who was stranded at the police station. Remembering my mentor's comments about kindness, consideration, and making friends in this time of crisis, I offered to run her home. In her difficulty, she was beyond pleased with my offer. So much so that, on arrival, she offered me a fiver for the trip: generous, even if I'd had a meter running. Surprised but more amused, I firmly declined her offer and told her I was glad to have been of service. I like to think she remembered that. From the warmth of her smile, I'm sure she did. That little moment embodied pretty much everything I'd joined to do and brought back to me the wise words of PC Frost.

9 Freedom of the City

And, so it was that I was signed up to be let out on the city's streets unaccompanied by a tutor PC. After a quick chat with the patrol sergeant at eight weeks, it was decided I could fend for myself sufficiently to be released into the wild two weeks prematurely. I'd dealt with deaths, drunks, shoplifters, and a spectrum of other matters, convincing those in authority I was fit to fly: a bit like those young birds that can wing it but occasionally crash land.

For "probbies", being on unaccompanied patrol was both scary and exhilarating. It was an incredible eye-opener. There was an amazing feeling of freedom *and* responsibility. I was excited to be outside on a wet Monday morning

---

[22] For more information on the call for non-invasive post-mortems see www.saadfoundation.com

on the beat, the damp fresh air in my face among all the hustle and bustle of day-to-day life. Shirley was lively, with people shopping, talking, drinking, delivering, and generally making a living. It was real life surrounded by real people. The locals were not middle-class suburbanites with their affectations but the main working class, often from families who had been in the city for several generations. They spoke openly, plainly, and engagingly. What you saw is what you got, and there was a humour that went with it. There is an immediacy and rapport with the public that is unique to foot patrol.

Walking with a sergeant past a bus queue, he spontaneously addressed the line in passing to their evident amusement. "You lot look like an identity parade!" he jovially observed.

That kind of interaction doesn't happen from a patrol car, and it creates a feel-good connection. It makes the unarmed police accessible and humane. It's maybe the difference between a police force and a police service. And that is important for individual freedom and democracy… I could hear Mr Keynes saying.

There were the lonely who wanted someone to speak to and take an interest; the widowed pensioner pruning petunias in a small patch of front garden, shop owners stood in their doorways; happy drunks (it was morning) and those who felt so low in the social hierarchy that, for a police officer to choose to spend a moment talking or having a laugh with them, made their day.

The main road north beat took me past Woolworths, the Post Office, the butchers, and the bakers. It was the more commercially mainstream business area, more compact and busier, but generally more boring. To walk the main road south was to see smaller, more specialised, generally less profitable businesses, interspersed with flats, the occasional pub, adjacent takeaways and on-street car traders from the big dealership down to one-man bands, like Russell's "Rogue" Motors as I coined it, where the salesmen looked like they'd harvest your organs for profit if they had half a chance.

Some of these smaller car lots radiated dishonesty. They had an almost pop-up quality to them, as though they could vanish overnight, with their portacabins and wary, hard-bitten-looking proprietors. They still attracted punters willing to part with their money for a car that very evidently wasn't what it seemed. Dodgy resprays and remould tyres abounded. Cars with seats so worn they resembled Tijuana taxis bore the endorsement, "one owner, genuine twenty-two thousand miles". Had it added, "on its last trip", that might have been more accurate.

There was one motor trader who had a darkly fearsome reputation. Val Dromone was a rough-looking, intimidating individual who probably developed the tendency after repeated Mickey taking over his name at school, the full version being Valentine. I suspect his school record showed him sick on the fourteenth of February every year until he was old enough to inflict GBH.

VD, as he was known to the local police, particularly on the amusing daily intelligence bulletin, was the "Big Fish" in our admittedly small and stagnant local pond. He seemed to be linked to anything and everything vaguely sinister or properly criminal, although he was quite possibly connected less than reputed. He certainly ranked top trumps in the visible local criminal hierarchy, holding perhaps a disproportionately high standing through reputation alone. His shock of red hair had also probably been a playground talking point, as was his missing left hand, the wrist mysteriously covered in a dark leather sheath. Stories abounded on this loss: knife fight? East End retribution? Triad torture?

The theory of his hand being caught in a particularly tenacious till seemed to fit best for me. The truth was rather more mundane. As recorded on his police antecedents' history from an early arrest, it seems failing to pay attention while attending to a lathe during an engineering apprenticeship had led to a sadly cut short career.

VD's links to organised crime were hazy. He was the kind of local Mr Big who was reputed to have known The Krays. He wasn't present at the killing of Jack D. McVitie but had his hat, that sort of thing. A "legend" in his own lunchtime rather than lifetime, as one detective put it.

My first encounter with VD was during a search of his commercial garage. This was reputedly a kind of Bermuda Triangle for stolen luxury cars, where the adjacent docks and containerisation played a significant part in their disappearance in England and reappearance in places like Estonia. The day I was there, there wasn't a car to be seen.

A colleague had asked me to help in the arrest of a mechanic from the garage, who had committed the heinous crime of renting VHS videotapes and failing to return them to the store. The zealot of a PC had determined that this meant, under The Theft Act, that the gormless grease monkey had formulated an intention to permanently deprive, and therefore, there were reasonable grounds to suspect and arrest for theft. Yes, this was the level of activity the police routinely involved themselves in then. Today, you'd be lucky to get this level of resourcing on a robbery. Certainly, in the 1980s, the focus was as much on property crime as people, very different from today, where the risk of threat or harm predominates. Ironically, the police are more remote from people today than ever before.

On this occasion, though, there was an opportunity to try and inflict some minor wound on the bigger fish. After a search of the arrested man's depressingly drab domicile, which revealed just a few battered and dog-chewed video cassettes of dubious artistic merit, including one about a young lady called Debbie and her escapades in the city of Dallas, my colleague then decided to search his work locker and, by tenuous implication, the business premises itself. I was a little hesitant as I couldn't see that we had much (or any) lawful authority to search, but I went along nevertheless in a display of solidarity, and the man himself was happy enough for his locker to be inspected, for the reason that was about to become obvious: it was empty.

While we looked in the locker, it was brought to the attention of VD, who had not been present at the start, that the police were searching his garage. Abruptly, a man looking like an irate ginger pirate who'd lost his hook came marching from the street across the open garage floor towards me with a look bordering on homicidal. "Got a warrant?" He demanded.

"Err, no, we haven't," I replied sheepishly, hoping my colleague, who was the officer in the case, might take the lead. He didn't. Before I could explain the legal position that Gormless had voluntarily agreed to the search of his locker, which just happened to be on the premises, VD cut across me with audible clarity: "WELL, FUCK OFF THEN!!"

And so, off we fucked.

The local intelligence officer (LIO), previously known by the more passive sobriquet of collator, published a daily bulletin Monday to Friday. (For intelligence purposes, policing stopped at weekends.) The bulletin was essential reading for active officers, who hoped information they had submitted on a subject might make publication. A bulletin entry was like a gold star, highlighting you as an active cop. Our soft porn video tapes seizure did not make the cut.

Another reason to read the LIO bulletin was its writing style. To keep a readership (given some officers were reluctant readers and contributors), the editor tended to be sarcastic and, at times, downright libellous to maintain morale and interest. Any joke that could be wrung from a situation was milked to its full extent. "A nick in the nuts!" was the headline for a well-known burglar caught shoplifting a box of bolts and fixings from B&Q.

After the early eighties, some bosses started to see the litigious liability that might lie in wait, particularly with a slowly awakening concept of disclosure (the provision to the defence of information held by police relating to their client). As a consequence, the fun was policed out, artistic licence revoked, and facts became the order of the day, much like a contemporary BBC comedy show.

It was through the LIO bulletin that we all became aware of some information relating to VD. He had reportedly come into possession of a very large number of gold coins - South African Krugerrands, in some kind of criminal enterprise alleged to have been designed to defraud Her Majesty's Customs and Excise. Quite what patrol officers were to do with this information, I wasn't too sure. It was probably a good example of inappropriate sharing in a moment of excitement in the intelligence office, the name of which, at times, could amount to an oxymoron.

What we also knew was that there was a warrant outstanding for unpaid fines for an amount of just over £900, which had a power of arrest if the fine wasn't paid in full. The name on the warrant ... Valentine Dromone.

From the passenger seat of a panda driven by Cruncher, I spotted VD and some of his cabal standing in the office of his garage, which fronted onto Shirley Road. We quickly pulled over and nipped smartly into the premises, bracing ourselves for a typically warm welcome. "Morning, Mr Dromone, I understand there may be a warrant outstanding for you?" I said, adding helpfully, "Unpaid fines?"

I posed my utterance as a question rather than a confrontation. He knew very well he owed money and glowered at me with eyes stolen from the hounds of hell. We were confronted by VD and his gang of four individuals, who collectively probably didn't have a CSE pass between them, but all looked like professional boxers, one of them being almost a double for John Conte.

To ease what was an uncomfortable situation, I got on the radio and enquired as to the actual amount outstanding and whether the warrant had a power of arrest. I knew it did, but I wanted him to hear it and from somebody else. The controller replied that the amount outstanding was £953. This transmission wasn't secure and was heard by anyone with a personal radio. Slowly and with some brooding reluctance, VD pulled a wallet bulging with notes from his back trouser pocket. As he did so, a chirpy voice joked, with shocking impropriety, "Tell him to pay in Krugerrands!"

I was stunned at both the comment and the voice: it was none other than the station's new chief inspector, Ron Harbour, who was known for having a sunny and mischievous disposition. I took a deep breath, but Val either didn't hear it or, more likely, chose to ignore the comment, filing it in his tray marked useful. Despite the girth of his wallet, he did not have £953, and he had to awkwardly request that the gorillas in the midst trawl through their small change to create a sufficient pile of cash. Full of spite and barely able to contain his rage, Val addressed the Anthill Mob.

"Look at the eyes on the c**t," he said, implying I was gazing everywhere in his bereft hovel of an office in search of some great clue to convict him.

In the presence of a gloating Stan, the money was counted very carefully, and a receipt issued. The bundle of cash was reluctantly handed over by VD, accompanied by a look of intense hatred. Regrettably, there wasn't a gold coin in sight.

Pounding the beat at night is not for everyone. One PC was famous for his aversion to doing it and dealt with his fear by walking down the white lines in the middle of the road whenever possible. Another officer, who regularly volunteered to do station office duty on nights, found herself dubbed "the Olympic Torch" because she never went out.

I liked nights for the type of work; however, there is nothing enjoyable about going to bed when everyone else is getting up, especially on a summer's day. It's not particularly enjoyable to feel disoriented, or like an expired battery at four in the morning, so I often took leave on nights. This attracted the disapproval of Inspector Peel, who oversaw all leave applications and saw a request covering a night shift as akin to a dereliction of duty.

Of course, I did work plenty of nights during those probationary months as I attempted to remain employed with the constabulary. Most of the time, I was allocated a footbeat, usually on the main drag.

Walking slowly and carefully during the early hours in the alleyway behind the Catholic Church opposite the station, all was deathly silent and calm. You could have heard a mouse breathe. There was no one but me about—or so I thought. My heart leapt as I was startled by a terrible scuffling and banging to my right by a fence panel. As my eyes oriented in the gloom, I could see a rather fat and ruffled cat sitting precariously on a palpitating panel, looking at me with a mixture of fright and downright contempt. We had both startled each other and were now calming down, our hearts slowing, defences lowering, both trying to regain our poise. I think the cat found its quicker.

When the shift was overloaded with officers, outlying foot beats were allocated. On a very bad night, that could mean Millbrook Road. This was the main dual carriageway into the city from the west and mainly comprised premises in the industrial estates on the dockside and a mixed bag of houses, a few shops, warehouses and a church opposite.

The church was modern, with a sweeping concrete walkway rising up to an elevated double-fronted glass door. About midnight, I wearily plodded up the ramp to the doors, which revealed an inky black interior. As I came up close to the door and shone my torch into the darkness, I was startled by a face peering at me inches away. A burglar! He looked alarmed. And I knew him! He looked back at me, equally startled with his heart racing. I know this because it was my heart. It was my face. I recognised my startled expression, capped with my helmet. I was looking at my reflection in the glass. Realising I was, perhaps, one step away from being scared of my own shadow, I decided to keep away from the darker places where shadows don't show. Instead, I headed for the open kerb, bathed as it was, in the security of a lunar light. If it hadn't been a dual carriageway, I'd probably have walked down the white lines in the middle.

After my inglorious efforts at delivering a death message at Ashford, you might have thought I'd get it right next time. Wrong. The reaction in the practical of the dumb-struck wife had left its mark. At my first real attempt, late at night in company with Sue in Shirley Road, I was reluctant to state the actual fact of the matter and momentarily tried to sidestep delivery of the critical part of the proceedings: that the deceased was, in fact, actually dead. My prevarication didn't last long as Sue delivered a less-than-subtle kick to my left shin that resulted in me galloping along through the message like a prodded racehorse, getting us out into the sweet, tobacco-fragranced outside air in record time[23].

Once released upon the general public on my own, I found myself dealing with an incident where a widow in her late sixties had collapsed in the High Street and passed away. A close relative who shared her surname lived with his family fairly nearby, and I was sent to tell him the tragic news. Failing to sort out my words properly through stage fright, I stood at the door and started to trip out my befuddled lines.

"Mr Graddidge?"

"Yes?"

"I'm sorry, I have some bad news for you; it's Mrs Graddidge....." With this utterance, there was a sharp intake of breath, and he put his hand up to his middle-aged heart.

"Mrs *Phillipa* Graddidge," I added, with the rapidity of a machine gun, before I had to rehearse the spontaneous cardiac arrest procedure from Ashford's first aid

---

[23] Courtesy of the British American Tobacco factory in Freemantle.

course. At this tiny addition of information, that of a first name, he relaxed and was instantly flooded with a joy way beyond what one would normally expect in such circumstances. Understandably enough, as I had just performed a miracle: that of bringing his wife back from the dead.

Being a first-year probationer, I was at the mercy of officers who were police drivers to take me on enquiries. (A minimum of a year's service was needed to apply for a basic driving course. Possession of a driving licence did not equip you to drive the forces' meagre 1100 cc patrol cars.)
    Working across another shift, one midweek morning, I managed to cadge a lift from an early turn panda driver. A young, slim PC called Ben Taut drove me up to Lordshill to obtain a statement and return some property. Ben was quite a highly strung young man. It was this that no doubt made him an exceptional athlete. He had been moodily surveying the streets from side to side as though trying to convince me patrolling was a very serious business rather than just sitting in a warm car looking out the window, which was, pretty much, what I was doing right then. I was feeling happily content with life as we drove slowly through the traffic lights at Maybush, next to the imposing Ordnance Survey building. At this point, Ben's radar detected a group of locals loitering with criminal intent by the kerbside. On seeing them, he scowled, then, snarling like a guard dog on a short leash, and restrained only by his seatbelt, he leaned across me to hiss,
    "c***s," through tightly clenched teeth, with the venom of a vexatious viper.
    Initially, rather taken aback by his ferocity, I grinned and observed calmly, "Ben, it's only an old lady doing her shopping." The target group of Ben's ire comprised three people standing at a bus stop waiting to go to Sainsbury's. The windswept gang leader appeared to be about sixty, wearing a headscarf and holding an empty shopping bag against her mock sheepskin coat. I almost expected Ben to stop and arrest her for "going equipped to steal". Fortunately, we were past mid-junction by then, and the thought of a mug of tea as we approached the station seemed to mellow Ben a bit. Just to be on the safe side, I felt it prudent to recommend a cup of chamomile. On reflection, I decided... better not.

You'd think police stations would be as safe as a locked hut on a deserted island. Unfortunately, you'd be wrong. Petty theft could and did occur, especially where it involved another officer's equipment, which some people thought was fair game.

Just off the parade area was the locker room. We each had a locker with a combination lock for our stuff. These lockers would be inspected by the sergeants occasionally, just in case you'd carelessly left a mouldy sandwich or a difficult crime file in there, or indeed some property you'd neglected to place in the safe.

It was customary for an officer to place their helmets directly on top of their locker. I came into duty one night to see that the black band around my helmet below the helmet plate had been removed, and I was confronted with a row of very shiny staples. A "colleague" had, for some reason, felt in need of a new band and had helped themselves to mine. I remember being shocked. I was perhaps fortunate that there was an eccentric and inventive PC on the shift in the guise of Mark, who suggested to me he could do a repair by using some black plastic disposable handcuffs, which were just thick cable ties. True to his word, this forerunner to Dr Emmett Brown from "Back to the Future" (presumably, this would have been a prequel) fashioned a band using a couple of rivets in his workshop at home. The result was impressive, covering the staples and looking better than the real thing. Personally, I'd have liked to put the cuffs on the thief.

So, the pilfering of pieces of equipment was not unusual. This also extended to non-equipment items. Wherever there was a small tuck shop run on behalf of staff, there would almost always, from time to time, be some minor and sometimes not-so-minor subtractions. It wasn't unknown for the problem to be so serious that cameras were surreptitiously placed to trap the sweet-toothed and sticky-fingered culprits.

Patrolling on foot and perspiring uncomfortably in the sunlight of an unusually warm spring day, I passed my relatively new military-style pullover to panda driver Robert Wrench for safekeeping. A deadpan PC, who was usually completely reliable, he thoughtfully dumped it on the parade room table at booking off time without telling me. It then disappeared. Fearing I would be made to pay for a replacement, I pinned a "wanted poster" on the noticeboard asking for information as to its whereabouts. Shortly afterwards, I was approached by a colleague from another section who, fortunately, kept his eyes peeled. He advised me that a new area car driver on their shift, a somewhat arrogant and unpleasant individual, was proudly wearing a brand-new pullover, "nudge nudge, wink wink". I passed this information to my inspector, who acted with uncharacteristic decisiveness, pulling the area car driver into his office at shift change over time in the presence of the man's own inspector in a closed-door session.

It wasn't a particularly difficult case for the dynamic duo to crack, as (1) he was wearing the sweater, and (2) my name and collar number were written on the washing instructions tag in large block capitals. The sweater was duly returned. His "defence" was that he had "found it". No action was taken against him. Not astonishing, even though there was an offence of "theft by finding", which was used fairly often against those members of the public, rather further down the food chain. To be honest, I was surprised the jumper hadn't appeared in the window of a local pawnshop, given it was one of the officer's favourite haunts for tea and biscuits. These days, I suppose, I might have had the opportunity to be able to buy it back on eBay.

10 Shift Supervisory Encounters

A long-serving but newly promoted shift inspector joined us. In a previous life, Ron Gilet—who could boast a part Gallic lineage descending from Toulouse to Totton —had been a shipyard welder in Weston and who, like his fellow workers, had squatted over the yard's primitive latrines.

Having advanced up the social ladder by joining Southampton City Police, with its flushing mechanisms and warm wooden toilet seats, Ron felt he'd really made it with his promotion to inspector. He had his senior officer issue brown leather gloves. The trade-up from blue to white collar was a visible elevation, spoiled only by the translucent quality of the white shirts. These exposed his trademark string vest, which showed through like a docker's cargo net.

One of Ron's jobs was area licensing inspector for the High Street and its environs. He had to visit a number of pubs regularly to ensure that they were complying with the Licensing Act 1964. It was also seen as important that the police made their presence felt and stamped some level of authority on licensed premises so they did not descend into pits of vice and crime and become "no-go areas". Well, that was the theory.

In some cities, the police managed licensed premises very well, seeing the pubs out at closing time so that the normal task of going home seemed like an enforced ejection at the hands of the all-powerful constabulary. Most notably, I'd seen this in Liverpool.

In Shirley, the truth was, a number of the local pubs were less than hospitable and *were* pits of vice and crime, and, if not "no go" areas, were certainly places to tread warily.

One particularly notorious pub at the time was off a side street called Stratton Road. It's a shame "The Shield and Dagger" wasn't called "The Trafalgar". That way, I could have said the police were engaged in several "Battles of Trafalgar" at this particular establishment. Unfortunately, I can't. Actually, its real name tells you all you need to know.

Following this conflict theme, a colleague in Scotland told me of a pub re-named "Vietnam" by the police due to the battles that ensued at ten thirty closing time. At this point in proceedings, the clientele frantically fueled on double whiskies and beer "chasers" in the minutes before the bar closed. The colleague told me it was the only place he had ever been assaulted by a man with no legs: he had been struck a sharp, sly blow with a crutch by a vindictively inventive invalid.

Another pub in Shirley, with a less-than-family-friendly fun scene at the time, was "The Griffin". Of late, it seems to have been a decent local: after a period shut, it looks to have had a modern makeover.

One night, as I patrolled past it, I noticed a very large, thick, and sticky pool of blood on the pavement outside, as though someone had neglectfully dropped a couple of bottles belonging to the Blood Donor Service. There was no one about and no complaint made of any assault, but quite obviously, somebody had received a significant beating and almost certainly was sporting a broken nose or worse.

The Griffin may have been of Welsh descent, but if its name had been aligned with its politics in 1981, it would have been called The Celtic Castle and painted green, white, and orange. Southampton had a large Irish population, with a number who had an Irish nationalist persuasion. There had been IRA activity in the city, with a bomb plot and an officer shot in the Portswood district in 1974. IRA terrorist activity on the mainland UK was very much ongoing. To cut to the chase, police on the premises would be, in the words of Billy Connelly, "about as welcome as a fart in a spacesuit".

The exterior of the pub was functionally rectangular in red brick with a small concrete forecourt. There was a tendency for it to be fairly boisterous of an evening. It was into this hotbed of alcoholically nurtured nationalism that Ron felt compelled by duty and the ever-watchful eye of the chief inspector (who checked the license premises register carefully) to visit one Friday shortly after we paraded for nights. Quite why Ron decided on a Friday as to, perhaps, a somewhat quieter

Monday, I don't know. What I do know is that he collared me with a, "You're a tall young chap, you'll do," and proceeded to stroll up the High Street on his mission with me beside him in our helmets, raincoats, and leather gloves.

Inspectors normally wore caps, with, in Hampshire, black braid on the peak to differentiate themselves as "officer class", along with brown leather gloves. They had slightly heavier and better-quality trousers, which I cheekily reasoned out loud was probably double-lined in the seat. They also had helmets with coloured enamel on the plate to further enhance their position. It was a helmet Ron had chosen for this assignment, and for good reason.

Outside the pub, we could hear some muted noise and the murmurings of people talking. As we walked in, it was obvious the door provided more than adequate soundproofing, for the pub was probably eighty-five per cent full, with not a table or chair free and only a little standing room. To be fair, the clientele was as surprised to see us as we were surprised to see so many of them. Craggy, hard, middle-aged faces resembling scree slopes scowled at us over the tops of innumerable glasses of stout. To order a pint of lager top in here would have been an invitation to be tarred and feathered. We approached the counter, where Ron tried to make nervous small talk with a taciturnly uncompromising barman who had presumably never kissed The Blarney Stone. (And why would he? He was from Southampton.)

At this point, a long-faced Irish-accented man of no more than five feet four approached Inspector Gilet. About sixty, with the telltale fine red-lined cheeks of a committed drinker, he could have been the double of the deceased seafarer I'd dealt with. He had jaundiced eyes and was wearing a black donkey jacket, which, on surveying the room, was not an outlandish choice of overcoat in this particular setting, given there were so many of them present. It looked like a meeting of the National Pick and Shovel Association.

The man took hold of Ron's right sleeve quite firmly and, with a policeman-like bearing, said, "Alright, come on now, we don't want your sort in here," and with that led a compliantly bemused Ron towards the door we had just come in. I looked on with concern as I could see that this was not at all acceptable, except it was happening! I pulled myself up to full helmeted height of seven feet and started to move slowly across the bar, attempting to maintain as much dignity as the situation allowed by trying to give the appearance that I was choosing to leave of my own volition. This is more than can be said for Ron, who, like a prospective patient at a New York hospital without a credit card, found himself unceremoniously ejected into the street with me following a few seconds behind.

As he passed through the threshold, a rather resilient mini pork pie bounced off the back of his senior officer's helmet, leaving a smear of mustard as though he'd been targeted by a seagull with gastroenteritis. At least no one had laid hands on my rubberised sleeve and propelled me to the pavement.

We returned to the station in silence as though in possession of a secret best kept to ourselves. Later, I noticed Ron had made an entry in the licensing register: "The Griffin visited: all in order".

Sergeant Locryn Fox, a dynamic and charismatic leader, was holding court in the parade room. Elongated and mildly athletic, he had a faint resemblance to an aged Pablo Picasso, except Picasso had more hair, and Fox came from Falmouth. With his left leg mounted on a chair in Napoleonic fashion, he read from Force Standing Orders to the assembled cops from shifts and beats in an accent that would have guaranteed passage on the Mayflower.

There followed a discussion about the recent Brixton riots and the inadequacy of police protective equipment: Met officers had used dustbin lids as shields, and there was a general feeling that more appropriate equipment might be needed, especially hard riot headgear with visors, as used in Northern Ireland.

"And when are we going to be issued with these NATO helmets?" Fox demanded like he'd been possessed by the spirit of the very much alive Arthur Scargill, the leader of the National Union of Miners.

Looking at his almost bald pate, I ventured the reply, "Looks like you've already been issued with yours, sarge."

This amused me and, from the guffawing around the room, several others. PS Fox, however, was as touchy about his lack of fully charged follicles as I was lacking in the art of tact, and he erupted into action like a mini volcano, chasing me into the locker room. I thought he was joking. He wasn't. It was only my height that prevented me from being stuffed into my narrow but, fortunately, inadequately lengthy locker.

A few months into my probation, the shift found itself with an additional sergeant. Large and grave with chiselled fifty-year-old features and wearing a uniform newer than mine, former Detective Sergeant Cristian Dunt had landed, if, as it transpired, only for a short while.

In those days, it was the case that detectives who had blotted their copybook sufficiently (or detective's diary) found themselves "sent back to uniform", as a form of public punishment. Many uniform officers resented the implication that sending back meant the ex-detectives had come from somewhere better in the first place. This was just one dimension of a uniform versus CID rivalry that has existed since the creation of detectives in Victorian times.

Television doesn't help, as, in featuring serious crime, it glorifies the CID. More crime is investigated and detected by uniform officers than by CID. In TV drama, the distinction is accentuated by a uniform officer standing guard at the interview room door for visual effect and to highlight the importance of the detective character. In reality, PCs don't stand guard in an interview. Indeed, given stories of the occasional, somewhat irascible detective types from the past, it is probable they wouldn't have wanted a witness.

As to Cristian Dunt; his misdemeanour would probably have been down to one of two age-old problems for a detective: alcohol or women. Given it transpired he was teetotal, we were able to draw a reasoned inference even though we were never told quite why he joined us.

For the short while he was attached to the shift, Cristian was a beneficial influence on me. On his first night shift, he elected to walk together at a dignified pace down Main Road South. As he enquired about what I wanted to do in policing, I cautiously said I felt I needed to get more experience in uniform.

"Does a man have twenty years' experience, son, or one year's experience twenty times over?" He mused. I nodded reflectively and said nothing, but absorbed the observation, which has come back to me many times over subsequent decades. To be honest, I was quite touched by him bothering to take an interest in me.

Grammar school educated, he would read "The Daily Telegraph" with a serious disposition and, to my admiration, complete its crossword. "Dark man by a river in India?" he asked me one meal break, "seven letters." I had no idea. "Gorilla," he answered for me. "Rill is a stream leading to a river; Goa is a state in India." He then shook his head slightly, bemoaning in the gesture the state of education in the country as highlighted by yours truly. His level of mental acuity amazed me.

I was usually above tabloids myself and would sometimes bring in "The Guardian" newspaper. That tended to greatly unsettle the natives, who saw it as the equivalent of "The Morning Post" and consequently branded me a "red". The intolerance across the board for anything remotely left of right of centre, or vaguely liberal, was concerning. When I once declared I'd bought a book of Contemporary American Poetry (an unwise disclosure in retrospect), I found certain shift members twice routed calls to me from "The Gay Switchboard". As it happens, they weren't interested in American poetry either.

Not without a sense of humour, in the appropriate company, Cristian would often introduce himself in the following terms: "Hello, I'm Cristian Dunt. My father was a partner in a well-known firm of Liverpool criminal solicitors: Cunningham, Carruthers and Dunt."

Early in service, I was introduced to a troubling procedure: the crime of the "meter break". Prepayment meters for gas and electricity were a common feature in council-owned properties. Renters put coins in the meters to obtain one or the other.

The meter remained the property of the utility company (as they are called on a Monopoly board). The coin contents of the meter, however, were a different matter, with the outcome always favouring the utilities. If a renter's home was burgled, the meter forced, and the coins stolen, it was the renter's money. On the other hand, if the renter, short of a few quid or a job, decided to break into the meter themselves to fund a night of beer and bingo followed by a beef biryani, this money magically became the utility company's cash, and the tenant would be ruthlessly prosecuted.

Gas or electricity board investigators would arrive at police station counters across the land to hand in pro forma statements to the effect that they had attended a certain address, found the meter had been broken into, cash removed, and that the company supported prosecution.

Sometimes the householder would try and feign that a burglary had taken place to absolve themselves of liability, but these stories tended to crumble pretty quickly when they were unable to identify any point of entry. Often these were people on the lowest incomes, unemployed, and in financial difficulty. This duplicitous practice had been going on for years. I was troubled by it and asked Christian his views. His reply was refreshing.

"To be honest, Brian, what I do when they come into the front counter with those statements is, I say, "Thanks very much, mate, and then (making a compacting motion with his hands), I just throw them in the bin." If only more officers had thought of that.

Despite his obvious ability, Cristian remained a sergeant to the end of his service, leaving the shift to return to CID sooner than I would have liked. When I asked him why he hadn't gone higher, he whispered, with a hint of paranoia, "If you stay at this level, you're not a threat to them, you see."

I didn't really see, but I think he preferred the "doing" part of the job with the autonomy of being a first-line CID supervisor. He had too much energy, character, wit and love of being actively hands-on to occupy an office. It wasn't many years before I saw, in the weekly published Force Standing Orders, that he had retired. I was saddened by this, and I wrote to him. He graciously replied with his final piece of advice: "Just remember, son, never get married, and you'll be fine."

11 Hulse Road Police Hostel

I had been unable to get a room at the police hostel when I first arrived in Southampton, as it was full of young single men and not-so-young divorcing men. Some youngsters had moved in as probationers and never matured sufficiently to leave until the bells of matrimony rang, signalling their reluctant departure into adulthood.

Unfortunately for him, but fortunately for me, a probationary constable had failed to meet the expectation of becoming an efficient and effective officer and had been dispensed with, meaning a room had become free, and I could move into the constabulary's equivalent of probationary death row.

The hostel was located just off the city centre near the common. An architecturally uninspiring rectangle which seemed to emanate from the art deco period, it had three floors with metal-framed windows and stairwells at both ends. One stairwell was more tower-like. It was both a fire escape and access to an executive suite on level two that housed the offices of the divisional Chief Superintendent, who had moved there since I had seen him in less impressive, if more operational, surroundings at Southampton Central.

The building was used for several other functions: administration, management, scenes of crime, and, to the rear, there was a traffic garage. From here, traffic motorcyclists disgorged like hornets onto the streets. That is when they weren't sitting in the canteen drinking tea with their helmets mounted theatrically on their handlebars, as in the TV show "Chips". Most of the riders seemed to agree that, aesthetically, the bikes looked better parked in tandem in the rear yard than out on the public roads.

Motorcycle cops were a breed apart. Generally less uptight than some of the regular traffic officers who drove the patrol cars, their enemy was the weather.

Rain was hazardous, while the sun was debilitating for them in the heat of their leathers. The actual effort of stopping a vehicle, dismounting, removing visor and gloves and then trying to write a ticket seemed to discourage many, although one was renowned for his astonishing work rate and eagle eyes: able to detect a defective brake light at a hundred meters or partially obscured number plate on a bicycle laden Lada, bound for some family holiday campsite in Looe.

Supervision was reputedly lax. It was suggested this had led one overheated and frustrated officer to pop home one summer's lunchtime to strip off and take a dip. He lived one hundred and twenty miles away and didn't have a pool.

The Hulse Road building was a support headquarters and used to brief and feed officers on football duties. One frugal inspector stretched the definition of officer to include officer offspring and would bring the family in for lunch on the days he was rostered for a match.

The kitchen was old, although not as old as some of the staff working there. The tall Scottish cook, Glenn Marange, was a kind-hearted chap who, in a past life, made sauce but seemed to now spend more time on it, steadying himself between meals against the bar in the adjacent police club. He often seemed slightly unstable while cooking, and I had an abiding fear that one day I'd come in to see his legs sticking out of the deep fat fryer like he was an elongated Glaswegian fried Mars Bar.

Chips were available at all times the canteen was open, including breakfast. The food was similar to school dinners but without the finesse provided by Jamie Oliver.

Entry to the building was through a rear door from the car park, which had a numbered pad for security. Many a time, a befuddled resident was seen fumbling in an apparent effort to recall the code in the face of a level of intoxication that would have had Richard Burton mixing his metaphors. Often, in defeat, a resident would have to wait outside for someone more clear-headed to arrive or exit for them to gain entry.

Just inside, to the left, there was a laundry room, and beyond that, green marble-effect toilets that had an abiding smell of very strong disinfectant. Next was a small foyer. Here was a payphone with a Perspex canopy that afforded the merest amount of privacy for the personal conversations that naturally transpired between the young men who lived there and their girlfriends. (If any had boyfriends, it was, understandably, in those days, a secret.)

From the entrance hall, the stairs led off to the accommodation. A further downstairs corridor led to a room containing an ageing but sturdy pool table, strong enough to take the weight of two people, and another room that had a television with a few old armchairs, which would have been of interest to the Antiques Roadshow and were probably purloined at the end of the war from the RAF lounge at Biggin Hill. Further along were the main foyer and some offices leading around to the traffic garage. This housed the motorcycle section's low-mileage bikes and an assortment of car engine parts and panels belonging to some of the residents. At the back of the car park was a set of small offices and white Ford Escort vans belonging to the scenes of crime department.

Officer accommodation was on two floors, most of it on the first floor, with a couple of misanthropes occupying rooms on the floor above. These individuals were stationed outside the city and did not feel part of the social setup, so they chose to remain apart, not even using the canteen. I'm not sure what they ate: raw meat, perhaps. One, who to me resembled a mean-spirited Doberman, wore black leather gloves to work in the summer to complement his short-sleeved uniform shirt and sunglasses. Perhaps he'd been inspired by reading the Mussolini memoirs.

The hostel was a bit like the Hotel California: you could check out any time you like, but you could never leave. Two young probationers, who decided they wanted the freedom of renting their own house, found themselves in for a shock when the divisional superintendent, on hearing of their departure, demanded they return after just twenty-four hours of freedom, refusing to allow the move. Apparently, he was concerned about the constabulary's reputation if two young cops shared a house. It wasn't made clear if this was homophobia or worry that the two young men would have a succession of women on the premises. As they were both former cadets, this latter point was a legitimate issue for concern. (About this time, a Dorset probationer was banned from living with his girlfriend on the grounds that they could not live "in sin" as it would outrage the parishioners of Weymouth. He resigned in disillusionment.)

It's highly questionable whether an employer should've been applying such draconian control or even whether it was lawful. However, the force had considerable control over probationary officers, who themselves seldom knew their rights or, indeed, rarely believed they had any, particularly given the way they were treated. Because of this, the organisation tended to get away with quite a lot, including, it seemed, false imprisonment. Another officer, out of probation, applied to leave the hostel but had to remain because the force would have to pay him rent allowance if he left: a cost it did not feel it needed to incur, given it had given him a broom cupboard-sized cell to live in, within an operational building (admittedly with running water). What it didn't do was compel married officers to move into police accommodation when it was available, and for a very good reason: there would have been uproar.

Rent Allowance was money given to officers towards the cost of renting a home and was a throwback to an age when officers couldn't afford to be owner-occupiers, rather like today. It was linked to the rateable value of a home: the higher the rates, the higher the allowance. As pay improved, it was no surprise when it was eventually frozen and ultimately phased out. For a single man or woman in the early eighties, it was a flat rate that the Constabulary was very obviously not keen on paying.

From my perspective, I was happy enough to be out of my vegetarian digs and amongst other young men who shared roughly the same classical outlook and interests: those of wine, women and song. In fact, if we were to substitute lager for the wine and football and snooker for song, that would have been closer to the mark.

During the time I lived in the hostel, like in my digs, I kept all my clothes in a suitcase which lay on the floor. For some reason, I was never particularly keen on the bare, rough-cut wooden chest of drawers or the unappealing, bleak cupboard that was made available to me.

The bedrooms in the hostel were certainly accurately described as basic. They comprised a single bed, a wash basin with mirror, a small table with a metal wooden-backed chair, a grey metal waste bin, a set of drawers, possibly pilfered from a prisoner of war camp, ancient orange sackcloth curtains, and that was about it. As to the small wash hand basin, this was so often the alternative to tiptoeing down the corridor to the WC in the wee small hours. Especially on a Friday or Saturday night, you could hear running taps and the sound of quietly burbling water in the pipe work, like a soothing, if somewhat polluted, hillside brook. It may sound primitive, but I console myself that this was merely the forerunner of the much-coveted "en-suite" of the 1990s.

The floors were dark-tiled and pitted. The walls were off-white, although it was okay for officers to redecorate if they wished. The styling was very much in line with that of the residential establishments run by Her Majesty's Prison Service. There was a fine line between being a resident and an inmate, given the environment and regime. Premier rooms were at the front of the building, facing the road and the police club. The standard rooms looked onto the car park at the back and the bins.

On the day I took possession of my first and standard room, I found it depressingly empty and dreary. It spoke to me of deeds I didn't want to imagine from the two or more decades before. Lying on the metal mesh sprung base of the single bed was a pitifully thin and over-exercised mattress. The standout feature of this was the multi-layered stain that spoke of the exploits and excesses of previous occupants, some of whom, it would appear, had a history of not making it to the sink. It was not a pretty sight. My first job was to cocoon the pummeled and flaccid mattress in several layers of stiff cotton sheets, which were, thankfully, white, starched, laundered and changed weekly by the cleaners.

Midway down the dimly lit corridor before the fire door was a small ironing room and, off that, a further room with showers and one cubicle containing a bath, beside which was a small, ancient grey cloth and a tin of powdered bleach. A large white urinal ran down the wall below a window that faced out to the car park, with kitchen bins directly below.

As the kitchen's large steel bins were uncovered, there was usually a swarm of excited flies that oscillated between them and the urinal above, not knowing which was more inviting. Usually, after some deliberation, the flies opted for the urinals, especially in the summer.

On the upside, from the rear rooms, there was a pleasant view across the car park to the long garden of the nurse's home next door. It has to be said that the only thing of note I spotted in it that was vaguely foxy was an actual family of foxes; two adults and cubs that frolicked in the late summer afternoon sunshine without a care in the world.

I told this heart-warming fox story to a colleague. He relayed a similar tale told to him. A very young PC had been doing pretty much as I had, leaning on the window ledge of his hostel room early one morning, watching the world go by. Of particular note was a sweet, if loudly singing black and white bird that was dancing on the far wall, framed by the greenery of the trees beyond and a hazy spring sunlight.

This magical magpie moment was interrupted by a dull thud. The bird froze as if startled, then dropped like a Norwegian blue parrot, stone dead. The bewildered boy, trying to make sense of the avian assassination he had just witnessed, stuck his head out of the window and glanced up just in time to see the long black barrel of an air rifle retract with the slow, deliberate self-satisfaction of a sleep-deprived murderer not long in off from nights.

Like most of the residents, I used the ironing room to prepare my uniform, but it was also used for one's own clothes. On a Friday evening, a group of us was preparing to go out. We were chatting through open doorways as we got ready when I heard a groan of anguish followed by a shout of perplexed anger. "What fucking stupid twat has done this?"

Intrigued, I popped out into the corridor to see what the commotion was about. Jim Oldman, the hostel's longest serving resident and the wearer of pristinely ironed white shirts of dazzling luminosity, was holding one of his prized garments, across which was a broad and very black stripe.

"That looks like boot polish, Jim," I offered helpfully.

"It fucking well *is* boot polish!"

Other residents arrived on the scene. One, uncharitably nicknamed Jethro,[24] after the kindly but naive character from "The Beverly Hillbillies", looked guiltier than the others. (This isn't the best moment to mount a defence for him.)

"Sorry, that was me." He confessed. "I was trying to bull my boots."

We were all stunned at this revelation. It transpired that our inventive housemate had tried to shortcut the laborious process of boot bulling—the classical procedure of spit and polish and twenty minutes or so of manual buffing, by coming up with an alternative labour-saving process: iron the polish on. Not only had it ended in abject failure, but (Jim's description), "the dozy c**t" had neglected to clean the iron's plate after the aborted attempt. A trip to Burton Menswear, anyone? That shirt was not going to be revived.

The poor state of the accommodation stimulated in me a sense of moral outrage, and I embarked on a campaign to achieve social justice. Over the next few weeks, I was in communication with the divisional administration manager, an ex-army officer resplendent in a bow tie and tweed and reminiscent of Siegfried Farnon from the TV series, "All Creatures Great and Small."

Mr Murgatroyd, to his credit, indulged my whinging and agreed to an inspection of "exhibit A" in my case against the constabulary: the state of the mattress it expected me to sleep on. This was after I persuaded him to authorise the purchase of some fly spray so that we could, if not eliminate, at least control, the spread of disease in the building's toilets and canteen.

---

[24] The Beverly Hillbillies: an American television comedy show broadcast on CBS from 1962 to 1971.

Despite his colourful colonial and military past, which I speculated boasted foot rot in Rhodesia, given he had a slight limp, he was shocked at the state of the beds and, probably wisely, decided to dispose of the evidence. An irrepressibly witty and charming man, he benevolently ordered new mattresses for all the quarters. These were about six times thicker than the old ones and almost certainly did immeasurable good to the backs and social lives of many of the inhabitants, who, of course, were strictly prohibited from having any visitors in their rooms. This was an instruction that was universally ignored. Women were spirited up and down the stairs from the car park with great stealth and greater rapidity. There was, however, for some, the "walk of shame".

The morning after the night before at a city night spot, a crumpled and pale young beau would have to escort his, by now slightly dishevelled "girlfriend" for the night across the car park to an escape vehicle, while under the humiliating scrutiny of the tea-slurping motorcyclists, who would examine bodywork and construction with unnervingly professional eyes.

On rapidly entering the car, sun visors would descend, and the couple would make a hasty exit. For the inexperienced young resident who had made the mistake of not checking his calendar, there was the less-than-enviable walk on a late Saturday morning in front of an audience of hundreds of male officers awaiting football deployment. If she saw you again after that, she *really* liked you.

The inhabitants of the hostel were varied. Some were like me, young nineteen-year-olds having left home for the first time and still taking their laundry back, if not to their mothers, then at least to their mother's washing machines.

Others were older and more long-termers who just liked the ease, if not comfort, of hostel life and hadn't come to terms with the fact that one day they might require a mortgage and a place of their own. Others were between accommodation and partners.

There was a steady flow of divorced, divorcing and separated men whose personal circumstances at home had deteriorated to the point that they were obliged to take a room in the hostel. It was quite a drop in status for a mature man in his thirties or forties to find he was dossing in the policing equivalent of a hall of residence. Even second-year students tend to have a place of their own.

Some of these older men would maintain their self-esteem and stand apart from the younger hostel residents, while others would be born-again twentysomethings and come out clubbing and drinking, often assuming the role of ringleader, and giving some behavioural insights into why their relationships might have fallen apart in the first place. Some presented an avuncular kindheartedness and shared beneficial wisdom with their younger charges. Overall, they were not ideal role models.

Where some of these men chose to remain aloof, they were still motivated to have a degree of human contact during the day as an alternative to the depressing highlight of watching rivulets of rain run down the large casement windows of their room, like the tears of an abandoned child. Occasionally, they would appear in the canteen for a cup of tea in the hope of a bit of company. A hostel bedroom could be depressingly isolating, especially if you had just arrived from a house that had contained the warmth of a wife, children, dog, double bed, and your own toilet.

Gathered around a Formica table on the uncomfortable light wood and metal chairs that littered the tiled floor of the dining area, a well-built young constable was recounting, to a mixed-age group of generally enthusiastic listeners, an experience with a young woman he'd encountered at a club on a night out.

She'd taken him back to her bedsit, which did not have a bathroom (or en-suite, as they didn't exist back then). He'd awoken from an intoxicated slumber to see her in the semi-darkness, squatting above a sink full of dirty plates and cutlery, giving them, what can only be kindly described as, a pre-rinse.

Although this story of lowlife, which even Jeffrey Bernard[25] might have thought twice about disclosing, was met with considerable astonished amusement from the majority; one forty-something detective, for the time being in residence pending a decree nisi and the sale of his three-bed semi in suburbia, had an eruption of outrage, fueled by alarm, which, was probably a justifiable reaction to the combined situation, location and conversation he was temporarily forced to be party to. Clean cut, clean shaven, clean smelling, and with a dress sense majoring on cream and creases, he exploded,

"If I catch something off a toilet seat as a result of what you've been up to, you dirty bastard..."

We were surprised by his incandescent reaction, and the storyteller felt suitably chastised, regretting he'd spoken. I was still chuckling over the image of the silhouette crouched beside the draining board. For the boys, it was the banter of the barrack room. For the detective, it was sodom and gonorrhoea.

Occasionally, officers from other forces would call into Hulse Road to eat. Sometimes these would be members of a driving school from another region,

---

[25] Writer of the "Low Life" column in The Spectator magazine 1978-1997.

where an instructor and three students on a fast-driving course would arrive to refuel and share gossip about the state of affairs in their respective forces. They would usually arrive on a Wednesday lunchtime when the one decent meal of the week was served: curry.

There was a category "A" prison nearby on the Isle of Wight called Parkhurst[26]. Category "A" prisoners were those deemed the highest risk to the public. Many were career criminals with the clout to organise a violent escape, and as a result, were moved in high-speed prison vans with higher-speed armed police escorts. Some bigger forces had dedicated prisoner escort groups who combined this work with royalty and VIP protection.

Often, the prisoner in transit would be lodged at the city centre lock-up while the escorting officers had a "refreshment break". These officers from far afield would arrive bearing guns and tales of policing from London and the urban centres of the north.

One particular group of eight from Merseyside sat around their pie, beans and chips, somewhat dismayed at the shortage of condiments in the southern regions of Britain. This led one chubby, cheerful member of their group to break into a reflective Liverpudlian monologue as though writing to a newspaper agony aunt.

"Dear Madge, I came home from work this evening to find the wife missing; the kids were missing, and all the furniture was gone. All there was in the middle of the living room floor was a bottle of brown sauce. Does this mean goodbye?" Sitting beside them, I splattered baked beans across my plate in a guffaw of mirth. One lodged in my left nostril like a negligently discharged bullet.

A skinny and intense Merseyside officer in an overly large anorak, who sported a stereotypical macho moustache and a dark curly perm that made him a Terry McDermott double, told me how they'd spotted some Liverpool villains a few minutes before arriving at the canteen and "turned them over" in a very Merseyside Police manner. The villains were bemused, firstly by the style of the policing interaction and secondly, when they noticed the badge on the police car. They were left with the belief they had been followed all the way from Wavertree.

Around this time, you might have thought that criminals might well have amounted to Merseyside's chief export. Mass youth unemployment and the opportunity to claim benefit anywhere in the "search for work", or for some, search for easy pickings, meant many young people from the north chose to move south, and very quickly, large numbers of individuals who were small-time

---

[26] The prison was downgraded to category "B" after three prisoners escaped in 1995.

criminals back home became big time villains in Bournemouth, Brighton and just about every other seaside town you could name including, as a colleague observed to me tongue in cheek, one or two of the less discerning who had ended up in Portsmouth.

The Secretary of State for Employment, Norman Tebbit, had made a speech extolling the virtues of getting on your bike to look for work. Some took it literally and, enthused with Thatcherite entrepreneurial enterprise, took someone else's bike, along with their car and the contents of their house.

Although the inmates of the hostel were known to one another and friendly, the fact was, we were all on one of four shift patterns, which meant there were some guys you barely ever saw, as when you were awake, they were asleep. You tended to socialise with the officers from your station or other city stations who were on the same roster as you.

The shift patterns in those days were pretty dire and were not designed for health, safety or longevity. After a Saturday 2-10 p.m. shift, we'd be back on duty at 6 a.m. This didn't prevent us from going out to a club or party and then returning in the early hours to grab three or four hours of sleep before work on the Sunday early turn, praying nothing would happen.

No surprise, patrol cars were little in evidence on the streets before ten if the occupant could manage it. One who didn't manage it apparently "blacked out" for some inexplicable reason. He was found with his vehicle stationary, up against a traffic light. Maybe he just couldn't find a colour he liked.

Sunday mornings were, of course, notoriously quiet, as the city itself slept or recovered from the night before; however, that couldn't be relied upon. As it was usually quiet on a Sunday morning, the shift would congregate at 11 a.m. after meal breaks. These meetings tended to be somewhat tedious gatherings of the duty inspector, sergeants and available constables for something described as "prayers".

One very young, gullible constable was convinced by his shift that "prayers" were a religious ceremony and that, as the new probationer, he had to read a lesson. Suitably nervous at performing before senior officers and peers, he practised every day for a week before standing up at the appointed hour bearing a Bible the size of a telephone directory. He then started reading a sermon in a halting and somewhat shy voice. The quizzical and indeed alarmed looks from some, allied to the less than stifled laughter of others, conveyed to him that he had indeed been well and truly had. Funny, perhaps, unless it was you.

"Prayers" was the name given to the shift meeting as it was on a Sunday morning, simply because it was the quietest time to hold it. There was certainly no democratic debate, generally just a monotone monologue from the inspector, who would read through the week's "routine orders", comprising details of promotions, postings, policy and procedure changes and new legislation that might affect us. This process was designed to ensure we were kept up-to-date, and it was quite effective.

On one particular "prayers", I was having difficulty staying awake. This was a problem that I had encountered a few times, and not just on early turn. Driving along the motorway after nights, the nearside rumble strip was particularly helpful in keeping me on the carriageway and semi-conscious. My nodding hound impression that morning was hugely humorous to the colleagues sitting opposite, who related that the inspector, fortunately not our shift inspector, but one with a distinct love of his own voice, had looked on disapprovingly, but my jerking back to consciousness every few seconds had saved me. The end of the shift could not come quickly enough, nor the opportunity to lie down on my new thick blue mattress.

There was a slow, steady churn of residents at Hulse Road, with a few long-termers, one or two who were notable for their eccentricities.

"Jumper" Jackson had previously raced his MG Midget until a collision with a kerbstone led to it inverting like a crocodile in a death roll. Fortunately, "Jumper" survived the event, even if the car didn't. This brush with death made him re-evaluate how he chose to live his life, and so he elected to get a safer hobby and took up parachuting.

"Jumper" would crouch in the open metal frame of his first-floor window while simultaneously holding the frame and a conversation. He had the unnerving habit of making you feel he was getting bored with you as, partway through listening, he would launch himself into mid-air and vanish, practising a parachute landing on the grass at the front of the building, occasionally offending the groundsman by missing his target and landing in the marigolds.

A connoisseur of grain whiskey, he had installed an optic above his bed. With that, a mini fridge for his beer, and the room's wardrobe for his parachute, his needs in life were pretty much met, especially when the occasional tandem jump with his girlfriend was added to the equation.

"Sinn Féin" Shaughnessy was, unsurprisingly, of Irish descent. He also seemed somewhat confused. A Northern Irish catholic from Bangor who had previously been in the military, he had a Union flag draped over the armchair he had brought into his chamber. He could be described as fairly conservative in his politics, given the pictures of a Waffen-SS Stormtrooper he proudly displayed on his bedroom wall. Actually, he exhibited absolutely no political interest or neo-Nazi predilections other than supporting the existing government. In my opinion, he was just over-inspired through reading too many Sven Hassel books. I quite enjoyed reading "SS General" myself.

For added complication, Sinn Féin seemed interested in Shinto warriors and kept a Japanese ceremonial sword in his room. "Sinn Féin" was, of course, a term never used to his face, but it seemed to amuse his cohabitees. His name was Sean, which matched his almost white, skinhead hairstyle. Sean thought vegetables were the spawn of the devil and only ate meat with potatoes (A stereotype perhaps, but…)

This diet had repercussions. One morning, I entered his room when he was still in bed, unsurprisingly, alone. If I'd been smoking, there would have been a methane-induced explosion. If he had kept a canary, it would have been feet up on the cage floor, stiffer than an egret's erection. Before I even greeted him, I asked immediately, "Can I open your window?" Ideally, I'd have liked to have sledge-hammered the entire wall out.

Sinn Féin had an air rifle and, when the feeling took him, would engage in target practice in the corridor, aiming for the fire door sign midway down. He wasn't inclined to announce these live-fire exercises or appoint a marshal, as Jethro found out one Sunday morning. A .22 projectile whizzed past his ear and embedded itself in the fire door as he emerged from the kitchen holding a now-empty mug, the hot contents of which were spreading down his trousers and over the floor. (At least, I think it was the contents of the mug.) Moments before, Jethro had been playing his music fairly loud, to Sinn Fein's irritation, and so it was conjectured the door might not have been the actual target.

The TV room was a place where residents could occasionally get together. The two favourite films watched regularly were "Mad Max" and "Animal House", the latter of which we all considered hilarious. As a group of us sat in ancient Biggin Hill easy chairs watching John Belushi, Sean walked in wearing a bandana, making him look like a Japanese ceremonial warrior. It wasn't the headgear that cemented the look; rather, it was him holding his Samurai sword. As we looked at him in bemusement, he raised the sword and, with a mock oriental scream copied from some third-rate war film, brought the sword down with the speed and ferocity of Anne Boleyn's executioner. His victim was a cheery Devonian from

Dawlish whose parents owned a dairy farm and who, therefore, went by the nickname of "Pasteurised" Pete. "Pasteurised" sat in his nineteen-thirties chair, his arms on the beech wood supports on either side of him. Normally a constant giggler, his face was drained by shock as he looked down to where the sword had embedded its blade deep into the wood of the armrest, just millimetres from severing his right forearm.

"Fuck me, Pasteurised, that was nearly the end of your sex life!" observed Oldman, failing to appreciate the potential seriousness of the incident. Or maybe he did.

"Feels like somebody else's doing it if you use your left hand," observed Jumper helpfully, no doubt breaking from a fantasy about leaping off a pylon or suspension bridge.

With that, we cautiously resumed watching a young woman slipping unconsciously out of a paper-stuffed bra while Shinto Sean, chastened by the near miss and his impulsivity, attempted to remove the blade from the furniture. It proved stubbornly and embarrassingly difficult.

Pasteurised had been top cadet, and if he lacked ambition, his girlfriend didn't: he was exhorted to study to pass his sergeant's exam even before he had passed his probation. Childhood sweethearts, I think he started studying for the exam just after failing the eleven-plus. He was like an Olympic athlete in training to win a gold medal. His room was littered with Baker & Wilkie Police promotion handbooks and Police Review magazine[27] exam questions.

To help himself utilise every precious second of study time to the absolute maximum, he had taped the definitions of offences around the mirror above his sink so he could memorise them while shaving. This dedication to examination excellence wasn't without its risks.

Shaving very early one morning, blurry-eyed and squinting in the illumination of a lone forty-watt bulb, he managed to, rather quickly and simultaneously very painfully, draw his Bic razor down the length of his isosceles triangle of a nose, rather than his right cheek. This was while trying to memorise the law on unlawful wounding. Thereafter, he bore the temporary nickname "Lager Pete", in homage to the Jamaican beer we all suddenly started drinking: Red Stripe.

---

[27] First published in 1893 to "cultivate the self-respect of the constabulary", it was the national unifying forum of the service. Its cessation of publication in 2011 was an undoubted loss.

A trusting soul, a quality that probably came from living on a farm in the back of beyond, he often left his room door unlocked. Spotting his leather-bound police pocketbook lying on his desk during a chocolate foraging expedition, I opened it to the pink detachable person check forms section and wrote on one: "Pasteurised, stopping another poor bastard who's committed some minor trivia like no L plates? Littering, with an overly sticky toffee paper? Let the poor bastard off, you fascist!" I then put it into his notebook at the last entry, abducting two chocolate digestives as I left.

On the Itchen Bridge that night, he stopped a moped rider, and indeed, it was for an L plate infraction. Opening his notebook to report the biker, he read my missive and, bursting out laughing (he laughed as infectiously as the clap at an orgy), he felt compelled to issue a warning to the bemused motorcyclist, who himself thought he had encountered the original laughing policeman.

At times, the social life was more demanding than the work. Starting in the Police Club at six, a drinking shift could extend to the closing of a nightclub at two in the morning. Various venues were popular on the social circuit: The Cowherds by the common, with its then collection of motor traders as regular clientele, and a downstairs bar called Goblets in Above Bar where the new fad for Australian lager was provided for, and everybody trendy was drinking Foster's lager or Grolsch: the unique selling point being less its flavour and more its flip top design.

In a street corner pub in Bedford Place, The Pensioners Arms, I spotted a wiry-haired, bespectacled man nursing a small glass of wine at the far end of the empty bar. He was crisply colour-coordinated in shades of ochre, set off with a striped scarf that embodied every other shade he was displaying. I recognised him immediately as I had recently charged him with shoplifting a bottle of vodka from Sainsbury's. His name was Elliot Pope. Well, that's the name he gave me. Had the result from his fingerprint check arrived back before this encounter, I would have arrested him, as the devious bastard had given me false details. They hadn't come back fast enough, though, as in those days, pre-computerisation, checks were done manually, and fingerprints went all the way up to New Scotland Yard and all the way down again by post. By the time I got wind of the truth, Tarquin Pump was nowhere to be found, and I had an uncomfortable five minutes being metaphorically pumped by a displeased acting Chief Inspector Peel over the matter of my being hoodwinked.

A couple of late-night venues were popular. A very regular haunt was "Fridays" nightclub in Vincent Walk, just about staggering distance from the hostel. Police were welcomed and (hypocrisy alert) let in for free. A night could be rounded off with a chilli burger from the American burger bar located just outside. As I ambled back one night clutching a bun, I saw on a fence along Archers Road someone had sprayed a harsh indictment of modern life in three words: "WORK, CONSUME, DIE". I had done two of the three that day. I started getting nervous. There was a genteel women's teacher training college around the corner, La Sainte Union College of Higher Education, run by an order of nuns. Somehow, I felt the spiritually voided wordsmith hadn't come from there.

Also, close to Hulse Road was a site that is now a housing development, but then contained the city's ice rink and, opposite, the Top Rank Suite. The latter was a huge cavern of a building, with an enormous dance floor and a galleried upper level. It was reputed to hold four thousand people, and although this meant plenty of opportunity and choice, it was easy to see a girl you liked in the crowd and then spend the rest of the evening trying to find her again. For lots of young women, there was, indeed, safety in numbers.

12 (Anti?) Social Adventures

The Indian restaurant with the diminutive ladle-wielding chef was located not too far from Hulse Road, up the city side of Beovis Valley. It was popular with hostel residents for the following reasons: it was cheap, open until late, and it had what appeared to be a malleable attitude to licensing laws. I suppose they were just progressive and ahead of the curve, applying the law pretty much as it is now.

Certainly, over forty years on, it is still in business, and I was pleasantly surprised (but mainly just surprised) that it had been voted one of the best Indian restaurants in the country a few years back. On researching the provenance of this information, my hunch was confirmed: the vote was made up of university students, who seemed to have applied most of the same criteria we had a generation and a half before. It was an establishment that, back then, especially later at night, had an eclectic mix: cops at one table, occasionally prostitutes at another and students and revellers from elsewhere.

A Pub, a nightclub, and then a curry house were often the contents of the evening's operational order. Despite achieving a bronze swimming lifesaving award and having possession of a first aid certificate from training school, the only time I ever had to save someone from drowning was in The Manzil.

I was sitting with five Hulse Road residents late at night. Pasteurised Pete was there and sober for a change as he was driving. (I can only assume he was on antibiotics.). He appeared to have developed a tic as he kept touching his right forearm, as though reassuring himself it was still there. Another, Matt Iculus, was a former plasterer from Plymouth with a George Michael smile and Andy Ridgley quiff, leading to the inevitable nickname of "Wham". He had uncharacteristically over-imbibed and was now becoming increasingly drowsy as the late evening wore on.

Also present was Laurence Peat, another probationer. Laurence had a penchant for gaming machines and had dark eyebrows, making him resemble a Thunderbird puppet. Lastly, there was Mark Thomas, an irritatingly successful hit with the girls, who had long eyelashes, long fingers and who knows what else. Mark could chat away freely until the food came into sight. At that point, he lost all interest. Pick from his plate at your peril: you'd get a fork in your finger.

Conversation had stopped on the arrival of the platter of eastern "delicacies". Onion bhajis, rice and various steel dishes containing essentially the same sauce with a different name depending on whether a tin of fruit or similar had been tossed in or not, were now on the table. Like a pack of hungry dogs, but with lower cognitive functioning, the basic instincts kicked in, and it was eyes down and all senses focused on the food and the business of loading carbohydrates in either solid or liquid form.

Fortunately, I was slightly less inebriated than the other three who were drinking. Pasteurised had left to visit the toilet. I had been vaguely aware of "Wham" bobbing and weaving like an amateur boxer with an apparent intention to limbo under the table. This movement, however, had stopped, and it was probably that which caught my attention and led to my life-saving intervention.

Wham had descended to a level where his entire face was submerged in a dark, rich gravy; his quiff caked in pilau rice and some mango chutney—the latter left over from his aborted attempts to eat a poppadom starter. A couple of bubbles had formed in the sauce by his nose, resembling some form of Hawaiian volcanic extrusion. As the picture became clear, I realised that Wham was likely to be the first police officer, if not human, to expire by drowning in a masala sauce.

Not on my watch.

I grabbed him by his hair and immediately wished I hadn't, as it was gelled more than an east-end eel. "Wake up!" I exhorted the involuntary Al Jolson-like figure beside me. (I guess I could have said Justin Trudeau, but he hadn't done his blackface yet, as he was only about ten years old.) I grabbed a serviette and partially removed the makeup, with the focus on averting spices from getting in his one, half-open eye. Luckily, he was breathing, as mouth-to-mouth was not an option. The general consensus among the group was that band of brothers in blue aside, his care was onerous and interfering with our eating, so, like an auntie abandoned in a care home, we rushed him outside and placed him in the back of Pasteurised's Peugeot, which was half-parked on the pavement.

Fifteen minutes later, back at the table and nearing completion of our banquet, with Mark battling with the remnants of a particularly resistant meat madras, in walked two uniformed on-duty constables, one the local beat officer, the other a special.

"That one outside with you lot, is he?" the weary red-haired PC sighed. "He's been sick down the side of someone's car."

We all stood up and gazed out of the restaurant's glass frontage, where Wham's head was hanging limply out of the car's rear window, supported by the frame, a trail of chutney chunder crawling down the polished white door towards the sills.

Later, aware of his inability to deport himself in a professional manner while under the influence of alcohol, Wham abandoned any pretensions to becoming a detective and instead took the pledge, embarking on a successful career in traffic.

It's inevitable that when out on the town, you are likely to be spotted by someone you have encountered professionally. When it's an attractive, smiley care worker from a children's home, it's a pleasure. Sometimes, though, these encounters can be tricky, and for some officers, can go very wrong. It's in these moments that how you have been in your dealings with members of the public can come back to haunt you.

Having exited from a city centre pub full of the joy of youth (or maybe a pint or two), a small group of young men barrelled past. The one at the front was a stocky, cocky, piggy-faced individual whom I recognised. On seeing me, he exclaimed, "Look, it's the handcuff kid!"

I glanced around as he passed, and he looked back, grinning playfully. It seemed like good-natured banter between two guys from opposite sides of the fence, but possibly the presence of half a dozen colleagues behind me had a bearing on the tone of that interaction. As I placed him in my mind, I realised I had dealt with him for car theft. I'd arrived to arrest him as he was about to go out for a Friday night. The deal struck was that he admitted it for a weekend's liberty and came in to see me Monday morning to sort the matter out. Very civilised all round. I recall he was very happy with the arrangement: he was on a promise, and with his looks, he wanted it kept.

In an Eastleigh nightclub called Martine's, I stood, looking what I thought was smart in a shirt and tie with a golden-coloured pin holding the collar together (as was the smart fashion of the day). I was feeling overly hot, though, mainly because I had chosen to spoil the cool look by wearing a somewhat straggly mohair effect sweater in an attractive hue of deep purple (help—call the fashion police).

I was approached by two lads, one of whom stood directly in front of me and, with his head cocked over with curiosity, said, "I know you, you're a copper." I nodded curtly, acknowledging the identification. Before I could reply, he added, "You threw me out the ground at the football."

Now on increased alert for trouble and wondering where this conversation was going, I retorted, "Ah, right, well, you must have done something wrong then, mustn't you?"

To my relief, he nodded in agreement, acknowledging the fair cop, outlining his offence: calling the opposing goalkeeper a fucking wanker with concomitant overuse of masturbatory gestures with intent to insult the opposition, which, when you think about it, is really why a lot of people go to football in the first place.

Having determined his ejection had been entirely warranted by the over-harsh standards of the day, there then followed a period of genial conversation about the possible fortunes of Southampton FC, after which he offered to buy me a pint, which I felt obliged to decline, despite my state of being hotter than a hot date on Mars. He then wished me well in my quest to find a dance partner for the night. He was kind enough not to mention she'd need to have an attraction for purple mock mohair and perspiration.

Opposite the hostel was the Police Club. Emanating from the days of the Southampton City force, this was a member's only establishment where the beer was cheap and the decor comfortably conservative. There was a large dinner and dance function room, ample car park and a snooker room with two tables where I constructed my highest-ever break: a lofty thirty-five. I was beating a hypercompetitive force and national police tennis and badminton champion. Seemingly unruffled by the experience, he glanced back over his shoulder from a glaringly missed pot to exclaim through a wide, forced smile, "We really must play tennis." Err, no, we really mustn't.

The club was generally a fairly busy place with a mixed clientele that didn't always dovetail. It was surprising the number of on-duty officers or admin staff you could find there from 11 a.m., either grabbing a quick drink or, very often, playing the two fruit machines.

There were several committed gamblers, some of them very young officers, who would stand in front of the spinning drums, hoping to align three cherries or whatever as they tipped a week's wages into the voracious machines. The attraction was completely lost on me. I watched the sharks that sat and waited until the machine was loaded and then, at the first opportunity, would play it until it was so overloaded it vomited an eventual payout—to the dismay of those who had primed it in the first place with all they had got. The sharks would bask in a sense of self-satisfaction after cashing in on the misfortunes of others. Not one of them was a likeable human being. A friend confided to me that he often couldn't leave the machine as he'd put so much money in, he simply couldn't afford to lose it. It seemed the hook was almost losing everything, then pulling it back. Unfortunately, there were occasions, such as when the club shut, that the machines had to be abandoned. Then it was a case of who got in first when the club reopened. Sometimes there was a queue.

On days off, I would often head to the club at eleven in the morning for a bit of snooker. Some of the more committed drinkers would be there or shortly afterwards. One such was Murdo McIntyre, a long-serving Scottish beat officer from Bitterne. This was the station covering the east of the city across the River Itchen. It wasn't part of "F" division and might well have been Stalingrad for all that I knew of it. There were certainly architectural similarities.

Murdo enjoyed a drink, and this enjoyment had led to a drink-drive conviction In the preceding decade. However, a more lenient approach to this type of infraction in those days meant he kept his job. Being a foot patrol officer, he didn't need to drive. Just as well, as the magistrate wouldn't let him. I would occasionally talk to him due to my family connections north of the border.

Murdo told me he had worked as a police officer in a small Scottish seaside town, which was close to where I knew Bill Street, my gran's neighbour, had worked for many years, also in the police. I was surprised, though, when Bill said he knew Murdo. They'd played football against one another before Murdo's "emigration to a foreign land", as Bill put it.

Back from the holiday trip north of the border, I saw Murdo and mentioned his erstwhile Scottish footballing adversary. In response, he said very sharply, "I don't know him," and the conversation was abruptly cut short.

When I fed back to Bill that Murdo had disowned him with the decisiveness of a disciple, Bill confided that Murdo had to leave his tiny borough force during the sixties due to what was seen as a minor scandal at the time: drink driving.

It seemed Murdo had moved as far away as he could to restart his police career in another jurisdiction, where perhaps his past indiscretion need not be divulged, given there were no computer records, and he might not even have disclosed his previous employment. I never mentioned the matter or connection to him or anyone again, but by then, our relationship was markedly more distant, and I could very clearly see why.

From 10 p.m., the club would fill with officers after the busy late shift, as they sought to unwind after work. There was sometimes an uneasy mix, with elderly couples suited, well-dressed and out for the evening occupying the same social space as officers in "half blues" and young residents of the hostel, who were comparatively big spenders in the club, but who often entered in jeans and T-shirts to the disgruntlement of the steward. He particularly objected to anyone coming in unshaven, as happened from time to time. Essentially, there existed a collision of generations, cultures and standards.

Within policing circles, there was a very conservative attitude to dress standards, as training school demonstrated. I joked that you could identify an off-duty cop by the fact that he was wearing a V-neck jumper and open-neck shirt, as, for most, this appeared to be about as wildly adventurous as it got.

It was quite fashionable among Southampton's male youth to wear colourful Fair Isle-patterned pullovers. They were all the rage and amounted to almost a kind of informal uniform. As a consequence, they were often worn by youths who got arrested. Stood nonchalantly in the club one night, wearing a burgundy version of such a sweater, courtesy of Topman; I was promptly accosted by a female colleague who asked me why I was dressed as a criminal. No stereotyping there then. (I got her back some months later after she had given birth, by, quite innocently, inquiring when she was due again, based on her girth. She wasn't.)

Some of the Police Club members weren't police officers. Often, they were members of the public who had obtained membership through a policing associate or relative. Some saw it as a form of social status. Maybe they'd been refused membership of the Masons, and to them, this was the next best thing.

With my shift after a late turn, I was startled to see a young man sitting at a table of six people. He wasn't a member, but one of them was, although not a cop. A month before, I'd been in the area car having just started nights when a 999 call sent us to an address where a man had been detained breaking into a car. By a quirk of good fortune, the caller lived in Foundry Lane behind the police station, the very road our car was on, and we were even facing in the right direction. We arrived almost instantly, nipping smartly down the road between dual rows of parked cars, blue lights flashing, and found ourselves outside the address within seconds. There, two men were pinning a third across the bonnet of the car he's been trying to break into. This was, of course, the very individual sitting in the club with a pint of Hofbräu lager in front of him. He'd been arrested and was now on bail. This was a bridge much too far. The senior sergeant, Len Stoves, was briefed. There followed a discreet conversation in the ear of the increasingly alarmed member, leading to the party and the unwanted guest leaving very abruptly. It was only then, as my indignation abated, that I was able to relax and enjoy my lager shandy and salt and vinegar crisps—with a pickled egg popped in on top.

The club put on formal functions on significant dates in the social calendar. Substantial numbers of staff from my station and others had descended. It was time for the Christmas dinner of 1981.

I was standing in the function room of the police club, wearing my best jacket and tie. I didn't have a girl to wrap an arm around, so, second best, I clasped a pint of lager. A small group of us youngsters were being talked at by a smooth, grey-haired lounge lizard of an area-beat sergeant from Portswood by the name of Cyril Styles. He was old school and told us to think less and do more, using the age-old line, "Yours is not to reason why; yours is but to do or die."

I'd never heard it before, but I assumed it was said around 1917, somewhere in France, in reply to someone asking, quite reasonably, what the benefit of leaving the shelter of a trench was to climb over barbed wire and run into enemy machine gun fire, way before breakfast was served.

Cyril was dapper in his dinner suit and bow tie and was living large, with a long and moderately fat Castella cigar held casually between the middle and forefinger of his right hand. Beside him was his third wife, who was late forties, platinum blonde, slim and wearing a thin but elegantly opaque to translucent royal blue dress. She looked composed and attentive, if slightly bored. They had, after all, been married at least eighteen months.

As he made his sagely profound observation, he drew deeply on the cigar with immense self-satisfaction, like a Hollywood mogul, putting his head back slightly and holding the smoke before exhaling knowingly, as though the silverback alpha male of a group of gorillas (those well-known cigar smokers from the Congo).

As he performed this affectation, he languidly dropped his cigar hand down beside his gin and tonic toting Mrs. The cigar had only recently been lit and, consequently, with the cutting intensity of a blow torch, its red-hot end sliced effortlessly through her chiffon dress as though the cigar was a scimitar. Instantly, half of the dress fell away, exposing not just her left knee but most of her upper thigh and lower hip. I'd noticed the dress was super clingy with no visible pantie line. I now saw that this was due to there being no visible panties. I admit to not having seen much in my relatively short life. I had, though, seen the Australian TV show about Skippy the Kangaroo. I had, therefore, seen a bushfire, just not one at such close quarters.

With a flurry of beating hands and a, fortunately, medium-sized evening bag strategically placed to cover the site of the minor conflagration, she glared at her deflated husband and declared coolly, "That is going to cost you." And it did. They were divorced within a year.

Away from the club and back on shift, Gareth Thruston was getting married. As it wasn't his first time, he was clearly prioritising hope over experience. Some shift members were getting excited. The betrothal meant there was to be a stag night. It was the biggest formal piss-up since the brewery trip that no one mentioned without using a confessional tone, accompanied by a nervous glance.

Rather than my favourite option of a pub crawl, others saw this as an opportunity for something spicier, and I don't mean a trip to the Manzil. The decision was made that a private function room would be hired at a fairly swanky hotel in the leafy outskirts of the city beyond Chandler's Ford for a "gentlemen's evening". This, of course, was a term where really only the evening part was strictly accurate. We were required to part with six quid for food and "entertainment", with beer being a separate cost.

For me, the out-of-town location was remote and posed a problem as I couldn't walk or bus it, and I considered myself way too poor to contemplate a taxi. I managed, though, to cadge a lift, although this tied me to the driver regarding the leaving time. I was unenthusiastic, mainly on the grounds of location but also content and the fact that I guessed (correctly) the beer would be rubbish. But it was a team event, so I was in.

Friends and colleagues of the condemned man assembled from various postings past and present and from outside the service. Lager and disappointingly gassy bitter were drunk. Chicken with chips was served in small plastic baskets and consumed eagerly, as befitting a last supper.

Chairs had been set out in the shape of a circus ring with a dining chair at one end. After his hearty meal, Gareth was addressed by his best man-to-be, who had assembled the night's agenda, and a few amusing words were said before the real action began. Gareth is known as a fast driver and therefore is a bit racy, says the man holding the mike, who I presumed was shortly to become his ex-best friend, as he moved focus to the coming "attraction": two young women, both of whom, in keeping with the circus theme, had big tops and performed a variety act.

The night's compere took possession of the mic. He was a stocky, blonde-haired man in his late twenties, wearing a shirt devoid of buttons from the waist up. Swinging, like an unrestrained ape against a knitted chest, was the obligatory gold medallion. For a moment, I had a flashback to Winfrith, but it wasn't him. The chest beater started proceedings by getting the two women, whom he introduced as "Hard-working young mums all the way from Bournemouth," to dance in a form that was, to some, mildly erotic and seemed to have been choreographed with some lewd version of The Arabian Nights in mind. There was chiffon, whirling, and arm lifts that exposed flesh that was inadequately covered on what was a cool night: outside, at least.

The two young women grabbed at onlookers in places the law precluded without prior permission, and a couple of the more eager spectators found themselves in the arena, where appetites were stimulated and lewd acts simulated. I watched a fat, balding man across the room from me, peering with fevered intent, and I could see sweat beading on his brow.

As I was sitting in a ring-side chair beside the dance floor, I crossed my legs in the fashion of laying my right ankle on top of my left knee, forming a kind of square designed as a barrier to repulse any attempt at forcing my participation in events. I found myself smiling broadly and chuckling at the absurdity of it all. My laughter was defensive: a definite attempt to keep them well away from me. However, it backfired as one of the women, by now almost naked from the waist up, came wheeling over, touched my knee, and, before she smilingly cavorted away, pleaded, "Can you stop laughing, love? You're putting us off."

I then realised that to carry this performance off, the punters needed to be, if not openly participatory, at least engaged. If it were seen as a comedy show, it would fail, cringingly. Feeling for her (as I doubt very much that she had this on her list of top jobs she wanted to do when she grew up), I sat soberly, knowing the threat of being pulled into the clowning was over for me. I felt intensely relieved.

At the end of the performance, at well past eleven, I got concerned. We were not packing up the chairs to go home. Instead, a plot was being hatched by the hirsute DJ, Mr Sweaty brow and a small hard core of onlookers that involved throwing a further three pounds each into a bucket for a "special show".

Seats were resumed, in my case very reluctantly (I felt like I was being held against my will), and Gareth soon found himself in a state of near complete undress while being lathered and creamed by the two women towards an ending that couldn't come fast enough for me but, with an audience in anticipatory attendance, can't come at all for him.

At this point, it was midnight: Cinderella time. The DJ reverted to his day job of pimp. The two exotic variety act performers transformed back to being "hard-working young mums" as another container, this time for tips on their behalf, was passed around by the compere, like an IRA bucket in a New York bar: the difference being that much less goes into this one.

Gareth was reunited with his clothes, but his dignity was missing and didn't make a return appearance for quite some time. I made a note to myself that if someone proposed anything similar in future, I should appreciate that the term "stag night" might actually mean "shag night".

Years later, I was back in that function hall, but this time buying some "fine art" prints: those that are by such well-known artists, the prints had the painter's signature emblazoned across the lower width, for the benefit of both the buyer and their cultured friends. Looking back, it's difficult to determine which of the two events ranked as the most vulgar.

As happens, officers come and go from a shift, and so it was with mine. Nick Church of the silent (no siren) area car departed from a seat that moved to one that didn't: he got a job in the control room.

He was replaced by a steady and eminently likeable PC transferred from Central: Donald Campbell, who hailed from that epicentre of the Campbell clan: Cwmffred in Carmarthenshire. Despite this, he bore no accent nor needed to break any land speed records, proving a generally enthusiastic and steady driver.

Also joining the shift was a petite and popular former army nurse, Flo Springfield, who had been moved rather quickly overnight. Rumours are unreliable things—unless they are accurate. In this case, the unverified rumour was that she had been found in a stock cupboard attending to a gash in a female probationer. This, of course, is completely the wrong place to provide medical attention and led to her moving station. Predictably, the spectre of anything other than heterosexual contact meant the probationer found herself out of uniform (again) permanently, although they did find her a job in another cupboard: the property office.

PC "Jolly" Roger Leigh arrived from Portsmouth. A big guy in his own right, his bulk was inflated by a bulletproof vest that he wore on duty, even when eating his sandwiches. Jolly had to balance the mild odour of stale sweat from the armour by dousing himself in liberal quantities of aftershave and body spray. Not an innately overly cautious individual by any means, Jolly had been the victim of what he described as a "kicking" in Cowplain, and this was his way of managing his future risk. From all accounts, Jolly had suffered a vicious assault. He was, of course, way ahead of his time: thirty years later, and all officers are wearing body armour. Body spray is still discretionary.

Gareth was to leave for a more rural area car posting where he could thrash along narrow country lanes, his neck craned over to the right, almost out the car window, to get an improved "view" around the next bend that was approaching at warp speed. He was never happier than behind the wheel. Robert Wrench cheekily suggested that he get one tattooed on his new wife's back.

Jeff Slocomb was a hyperactive and tense detective who was seconded (permanently, it transpired) to us on uniform from Special Branch due to personal difficulties that left him living temporarily with his mum and, occasionally, under cover of a bus shelter. He had a pageboy bob of yellow hair that sat like a jellyfish on a head, rather too old for the style. His tie was always hanging down like a rebellious schoolboy's. He smoked roll-ups almost continuously while buzzing around in a panda car, as though dealing with the problems of the world single-handedly.

Being separated, Jeff was always up for a pint after an early turn and took me to his local pub, "The Imperial" in Freemantle. The dark-wooded, partitioned public bar was always rammed with people he knew from childhood. Bearing parcels of fish and chips, we were greeted with a warm welcome and two white porcelain plates. We had to be quick as closing was at two-thirty, with ten minutes of drinking up time. These were days when pubs were for drinking. If you wanted food, they had crisps, nuts, or, in cases of extreme hunger, pickled eggs, and that was it. Oh, and plates if you brought your own. Eventually, Jeff found himself posted to jailer duties at central (pretty much for the stability) and where he found himself handing out porcelain plates to the prisoners.

Phil Duke was a bright and gregarious surprise addition to the shift, with a colourful choice of off-duty attire. Phil was another detective who had been "sent to uniform" as a punishment. His offence had been to be overly dutiful in intervening in a dispute between a customer and a publican he knew. The customer had been difficult and was ejected from the premises, but complained that Phil was under the influence of spirits that were not of the Doris Stokes variety. Phil became a respected ABO for a while as he engineered a shift pattern closer to that of his beloved CID. He was far too good a guy to be out in the cold for long and was soon recalled to the detectives, leading to him excitedly reviving his suspended Moss Bros clothing account.

Stan, a very hardworking shift stalwart, vanished for three months to do a CID aide to test his suitability in criminal investigation. Although possibly less than well-suited for some aspects of CID work, on the grounds that he at times exhibited the sensitivity of Oliver Cromwell, they decided to take him on. He actually found he fitted in very well.

13 CID

In the days when constables spent most of their working life on foot out in the elements, the prospect of better hours and improved working conditions appealed greatly. The shelter of the office, or the pub, from the cold and rain, was a great draw.

Detectives mainly worked 8-4 or, less often, 4 to midnight on each sub-division. One worked across the west of the city each night, like Norris Sharpe, who took on my first burglar arrest. They wore "plain clothes", with the emphasis usually on plain.

Suits had to be dark blue or grey. As sports jackets and slacks were cheaper, these were worn but frowned upon by the hierarchy as being too casual. Any attempt at sartorial self-expression was ruthlessly suppressed. You might look cool turning up to work in a cream John Travolta-style suit in summer, but you would be winging your way home to change pretty quickly if you did.

Detectives had access to "unmarked cars". These were strikingly bright blue Ford Escorts that were presumably less popular with the buying public and, therefore, cheaper for the police to bulk buy. This colour made the cars particularly conspicuous. As one constable observed, "Those CID cars stand out like a bulldog's bollocks."

So obvious were they to the criminally inclined populace, they may as well have had CID written on the side and bars painted on the windows. The fact that they had consecutively numbered license plates was a thoughtful touch in assisting the local villains in identifying them.

The CID offices were located on the first floor at Shirley station. There was a detective inspector (DI), three sergeants in their separate office, and around a dozen DCs in the main bear pit, which at times could be as noisy as the floor of the stock exchange if the right characters were present, particularly after a Friday liquid lunch. The workload of these officers was heavy: rape, robbery, serious assaults, attempted murder... the list of serious matters they dealt with was substantial. Surprisingly to the public, perhaps, a lot of it was child abuse work, both physical and sexual.

Each DC had a desk and telephone: even their own telephone book. No workbox, spread out on a communal table in the parade room for them. They had pocket notebooks like us "woollies" (a CID term of "affection" for their uniform colleagues in their pullovers), but unlike uniform officers, who had to record everything in them, detectives only used theirs for recording evidence. Additionally, they kept diaries where they recorded their daily whereabouts, including who they met and, importantly, how much overtime they had incurred and expenses claimed. Diaries were used to keep this information out of pocket notebooks and out of the hands of barristers who might examine them in open court and start asking about informants or, as the entries were more prevalent, visits to pubs.

It didn't always work in the brief's favour. One barrister seized a detective's notebook and theatrically read an extract aloud in front of a jury before realising what he was reading was injurious to his client's case. Declaring he couldn't read the handwriting, he hurriedly returned the notebook to the officer with a disdainful flourish, commenting, "Well, Mr Richardson, I suppose we will just HAVE to believe you." The jury did. His client promptly got six years for a knife-point robbery.

Question: do detectives influence TV depictions, or is it the other way around? "The Sweeney" had been showing to big audiences in the mid-seventies in the prime-time ITV spot of 9 p.m. on a Wednesday, depicting a culture of hard drinking, heavy smoking, and womanising detectives in the Flying Squad. The 1970s press reported on a corrupt, laddish, Masonic culture—admittedly in the Met mainly—which found itself investigated by Dorset and Hampshire officers in an operation called Countryman, which was derisively renamed "The Sweedy".

Certainly, some detectives tried to live up (or down) to the TV image. One detective used an adapted form of cockney rhyming slang that we concluded he had learned from the telly.

A DS was overheard holding court in a bar, "The one good thing about the Mafia? They look after one another." For some, the lack of a totally suitable substitute body to affiliate with meant they found themselves drawn to the Masons. Of course, the Masons were significantly dissimilar to the Mafia on at least one ground: they actually gave money away. They did, though, have a reputation, deserved or undeserved, for looking after their members. And they had a snooker table.

When it came to women, there were inevitably some lounge-suited lotharios who treated this as part of the job description. One middle-aged manager at another station, by the name of Andy Ruttingham, was known to have a predilection for newly arrived conscripts.

Paired with a slight and willowy nineteen-year-old probationer called Emily, I walked past "Randy" Ruttingham's office, which abutted a long stone-floored corridor. I glanced in and caught him looking up. As we sat in the dreary parade room moments later, I said, "The acting DI will be along in a minute." Emily looked at me quizzically. "Because you're here," I added.

Sure enough, after a minute or so, Randy arrived. He stood in the parade room doorway, lasciviously hitching up his trousers and pulling in his stomach while simultaneously pushing out his chest like a circus strongman. Emily was as coolly unimpressed as she was attentive. "Boss, your fly's undone," she observed helpfully.

There was a significant drinking culture (as there was in many professions at the time). Often drinking was linked, somewhat tenuously, to "meeting an informant". Pubs weren't very clandestine locations for this type of activity, especially as the CID's favourite pub was a short walk to, and slightly longer walk back, from the station. Nevertheless, many an evening's drinking, subsidised by expenses and sometimes overtime, took place on that pretext.

Some DCs did not partake. These tended to be the quieter, more approachable ones, who sat on a late shift completing paperwork with their sandwiches in a Tupperware container. These were the ones who seemed more likely to remain in the one marriage. There was a legion of divorced and separated officers in CID working all the overtime there was: presumably much of it being paid in maintenance.

They say all good things come to an end: bad things, too. This was a time when a conviction for drunk driving might not be career-terminating, especially if the right people liked you. A rural beat PC, who came off his lightweight motorcycle after a festive bout of "community policing" (community drinking), blew a positive breath test but kept his job when the chief constable declared, "I expect my officers to have a drink at Christmas."

A well-connected DC who fought officers who breathalysed him and then ran away kept his job. This benevolent attitude to intoxication and poor conduct found itself under increasing pressure as the decade progressed, particularly when the old chief constable, known for enjoying a pint himself, retired.

This was unfortunate for Ruttingham, who, treating a CID car as his own, took it home and had a minor accident with a cyclist on the way after meeting a female informant in a pub. (It's true, his diary said so.) Regrettably, for him, it wasn't the Mafia who did the breath test; it was the traffic department. He found he was very quickly dismissed into the world of private security, to a job identified for him by a supportive snooker partner.

It wasn't just CID that was part of a drinking culture. A uniform Chief Superintendent had a similar encounter with a breath test kit. Hastily, he took leave before resignation. On the door of his office suite was the sign, "On annual leave". Underneath, some wit had pencilled in: "At the Betty Ford Clinic."

Although overwhelmingly a "boys club", there were women in CID; usually one or two in an office. They were accepted, and some joined in the, at times, heavy social scene. WDCs (women detective constables as they were known then) tended to carry disproportionately high numbers of child abuse and sexual assault cases, in what was seemingly a bias along the lines of women and children were better dealt with by women. Many men found dealing with child abuse cases very uncomfortable, as though it somehow impugned their masculinity. In reality, many just didn't have the softer skills and sensitivity to work with this group of victims.

In the early 1990s, new shift patterns transformed policing, creating longer working days of ten or twelve hours and giving uniformed officers many more days off. No longer were officers wedded to the job. It also rendered CID work much less attractive. As more women moved into full-time work and families juggled childcare, fixed shift patterns with more days off have proved more attractive than a career as a detective, the status of which has diminished, leaving the significant shortages of recent times. Heavy, stressful workloads and criminal justice system deficiencies don't help either. In the early 1980s, though, the CID was a strong, well-funded department, and it had a great sense of self-importance. The work was certainly more serious, complex, and demanding, and DCs were free from petty discipline and had a high degree of autonomy in how they worked. Most were first-class officers recruited for their ability to handle heavy workloads and for their investigation and interviewing skills.

Most of my early dealings with CID were in writing with Detective Sergeant Freeman, who was exactly one of these first-rate detectives. Freeman was a conscientious and thorough officer with curly, sandy hair and a pair of thick-framed spectacles that gave him more than a passing resemblance to Michael Caine. I learnt a lot from him.

I would submit a crime file through the chain of command. I might have dealt with a shoplifter or arrested someone for assault. After a person is charged, a file is needed for court. Before it went to the prosecuting solicitor's office[28] (pre–Crown Prosecution Service), the file would go from me to my patrol sergeant, who would look at it and send it back with any observations or tasks to be done to get it in order. Back, I would send it. Normally, it would get through this submission to the shift inspector. Generally, their touch was light, but if they noticed anything, back it would come via the sergeant. Back it would go in again through the sergeant and inspector, on to the detective sergeant.

It was at this point in the pinball proceedings that DS Freeman was able to demonstrate his considerable investigative expertise by often sending me back upwards of thirty points to be attended to. Back the file would go through him to the detective inspector, who generally noted it, and off it went for court. It was eighteen months before I submitted a crime file and never saw it again. By that point, I felt I had arrived.

Incidentally, it was Freeman who mentioned the concept of invisible managers to me: managers who don't add value. When so many people are involved in a process, they often just note the file without looking at it, relying on it having been looked at by others. Unfortunately, if everyone in the chain does that, an unsatisfactory effort can get through. In later years, the bureaucratic chain was shortened considerably.

I was scared to enter the lion's den of the DS's office. If I could, I would ambush Freeman on the stairwell to query any of his points, quaking slightly at his not-unreasonable irritation at holding court mid-step as he was arrested from making progress towards the toilet. As my two-week CID attachment was looming, I realised I would have to move from consultations with Freeman in the stairwell to the detective sergeant's main office. I was worried. And not just about that. I considered my alcohol consumption was probably just about up to the job, although the appearance of being sober might be a bigger challenge. More pressingly, I simply did not have the kind of clothes needed. My sackcloth jacket from Ashford was just that and not really acceptable. An urgent remedy was needed, so I decided on action: I would buy a suit.

---

[28] Police prosecutors were based in their own offices but were often put under pressure to prosecute when the evidence did not justify it, especially by CID. This was a factor in the setting up of the Crown Prosecution Service (or Crown Cock up Service as some PCs called it in its early years).

Given I was not an off-the-peg size, this required a made-to-measure remedy, so off to Hepworth's in Bournemouth I went, where I was relieved of the gargantuan sum of one hundred and twenty pounds but provided with a fetching blue flannel two-piece that was ideal for weddings, Bar Mitzvahs, and parties, but probably not house searches. I was either the best-dressed person at the scene of the crime, or I had gotten lost on my way to a christening. One morning, a DC brought me a carnation buttonhole; it was a thoughtful touch. Somebody else considerately provided a copy of a Grattan home shopping catalogue beside my temporary desk. The temporary nickname of "mannequin man" was ascribed to me by another office wit. Sorry, I think I dropped a "t" there.

I found the CID attachment fairly tedious, as I had to traipse around, following detectives as they visited various banks and commercial premises to obtain statements about things I didn't much understand or had an interest in. When I wasn't watching someone else take a statement, I took a few myself, including two from a couple of lesbians. Polite and charming, I glided over any questions I felt might be intrusive to the degree that they confided to the investigating officer that they didn't think I understood they were in a relationship or understood much about lesbianism. Oh, to be so young and to be judged so innocent! They weren't right, but then, they weren't so far wrong either.

On my last evening, I was rostered for a 4-12 p.m. late shift. I was paired with a swarthy DC who considered it his duty to take me around the clubs. I wasn't reluctant to participate in this undertaking, given the administratively focused fortnight I had experienced so far. Exiting a club called Rumrunners at 2 a.m., after a thoroughly eye-opening few hours, during which my comrade in arms overshared somewhat regarding an anti-social condition that somewhat put me off seafood, there was a realisation that, at some point, if I could overcome the probationary hurdle, it just might be a career I could get used to.

After two weeks, my suit was mothballed, and I returned to shift to be reacquainted with the workings of a personal radio and the 4 a.m. job of putting out the traffic cones for football the next day. High life to low life: and all in a little over 48 hours.

14 Area Beat Officers

Matt Ramsay was an area beat officer. Pullover sleeves pulled up, exposing hairy forearms, and with his helmet set at a jaunty angle, he examined his look in the full-length parade room mirror. "Right, now, to go and arrest this bastard who has let me down badly," he announced to those who were present, doing reports. Matt was unhappy. It appeared he had to do some police work.

Apparently, an individual on his beat was wanted on a warrant. One of the few things an ABO had to do was ensure that warrants were processed. This meant either money was recovered or a person arrested. Failure to complete this fairly routine duty satisfactorily would probably, after time, involve removal from the beat. That would mean losing all of its attractions, and that was certainly something that Matt Ramsay was keen to avoid. He had "his patch", and he wanted to keep it. It was normally a pleasure to see Matt. He didn't come into the station much and, with his personal radio's battery problem, it wasn't easy to contact him. Fortunately, emergency calls weren't the provision of the ABOs, so if he went off grid for a few hours, or indeed days, no one really noticed. Rumour had it that when the stresses of beat life were too much, he'd decompress by diving in Dorset. He was even rumoured to do this occasionally on his days off.

The subdivision was divided into area beats, which aligned with a particular ward, each with its own identity. Each of the council estates, the sprawling Millbrook, the more modern Lordshill, and the older Shirley Warren, was an area beat. So was Fremantle, down by the docks. It had narrow terraced back streets, one of which perfectly framed the bows of the immense QE 2 between two rows of houses when it was in dry dock. Fremantle, like the other beats, had intensely local pubs. Uniquely, as alluded to previously, it had that strong early morning sweet smell of tobacco courtesy of a cigarette factory.

Panda car beats were overlaid on the area beats and were bigger. Area beats were viewed rosily as the bedrock of policing. Each area had a single dedicated PC. Unlike contemporary times, many beat officers spent most of their careers on *their* beat.

Some had been beat officers since the nineteen sixties, from their time in the Southampton City force, where foot beats had dominated in a time before the panda car system. After the amalgamations[29] in the late sixties, many had remained "frozen"[30] in the city and elected to remain in post for fear of transfer to some far-flung northern corner of Hampshire or the isolation of the Isle of Wight.

In those times, people tended not to travel great distances to work. Lots of officers lived in police housing. To transfer often meant a house move, possibly to somewhere more unpleasant, and the upheaval of a reluctant family, so many officers refused promotions or career progression, preferring to stick with what they knew and had. That meant many just stuck with the beat they knew and the place they lived.

Because ABOs were properly dedicated to their areas, they really got to know the locals. There were two great motivators to get to know people: rain and cold. "Tea stops" were police-friendly locations where officers could call in for a chat and a cuppa. Some were generic: those on the main foot beats where they could expect to see an officer most shifts, while others were kept secret, often by the ABOs, as a treasured oasis of hospitality to be cultivated like a garden and managed carefully. If the widow Mrs Kipling made exceedingly good cakes and liked nothing more than a weekly chat for an hour or so, it was not in an officer's best interest to share this information with colleagues. By cultivating contacts like this on a beat, an ABO could make life quite comfortable.

Some officers went further, developing relationships with those who could benefit them: the local garage, fishing tackle emporium, flooring contractors, painting and decorating suppliers, and the like. Often, real friendships developed, although some were inappropriate, like close contact with antique dealers or pawn shop owners whose adherence to the law might be, and often was, highly

---

[29] There were 128 police forces in England and Wales in the early 1960s. Many cities and boroughs had their own force. This was inefficient and bred local corruption. The amalgamations of 1967 led to 43 forces.

[30] To elect to freeze within one's previous force meant an officer could not be posted outside that force area e.g. Southampton City. Officers could elect to unfreeze for promotion or specialisation, but that meant the prospect of transfer anywhere in the new force area i.e. Hampshire (including the Isle of Wight).

questionable. It wasn't inconceivable for a friendly constable to come in the front door as a burglar exited the back.

The ABOs weren't an emergency service, despite several riding bikes. (This was more a reflection of the distance between their beat and station.) Their job was to follow up on quality-of-life complaints in slow time, deal with summonses and warrants, and maintain a policing anchor in their community. There were several perks to the role: shifts were 8-4 days or 4-12. No nights. ABOs didn't deal with road traffic accidents and could avoid prisoners and crime investigations that might generate prisoners if they wanted to, although one or two had a lot of "prisoners", as arrested persons were called.

When PC Ramsey was challenged about his communication difficulties and whereabouts, Matt adopted a less-than-easy manner towards supervisors and colleagues alike. There was an art in such avoidance, and there were several officers who developed brusque or aggressive attitudes to cover their less-than-dutiful activities. On other occasions, bare-faced humour or front sufficed.

A newly appointed chief inspector called in officers' pocket notebooks (PNBs) for a regular inspection. The notebooks had an index at the back where a record of those persons arrested, charged, or reported for summons for various traffic or minor offences would have their details recorded. This was where the kind of minor work known as "process" was recorded.

The chief inspector had noticed a considerable number of blank pages at the rear of Ramsey's notebook, implying that he hadn't actually done any process during the many months it had been in his possession (PNBs were numbered with the date of issue recorded. You would have a pocket notebook for a lengthy period if you recorded very little in its pages).

The chief inspector sat Ramsey in front of him and said sternly, "PC Ramsey, you don't appear to have done any process?"

Ramsey replied nonchalantly, "Well, you know how it is, Guv'; some years you do, some years you don't."

Rather like an assessment of vintage wine, this, apparently, hadn't been a "good year". Still, only another ten times twelve months to go at the taxpayers' expense until the completion of his thirty.

On another occasion, Ramsey was off sick with a bad back. He had been sick for so many days, it was incumbent on the duty sergeant to visit him at his home for what was known as a "welfare check". The idea here being to offer support to the sick or motivate the malingering to return to employment.

The sergeant was somewhat surprised to see Ramsey on his hands and knees in his front room, perspiring with endeavour, halfway through the laying of particularly attractive Pergo laminate flooring. He was even more surprised to find the on-duty traffic warden present, stripped down to his shirt and braces, emulsion splattered in his hair and across his face, as he painted the hallway ceiling with a gleamingly new extendable brush.

On another occasion, Ramsey had been detailed to collect a prisoner who had been arrested in London. He was going with a young probationer in the prison van and told the youngster that he should bring a "civvy jacket" as they might stop for a pint on the way. The excited probationer was somewhat dumbstruck when Ramsey drove out of the station, turned in the opposite direction to London, and promptly drove up onto a pub forecourt in Shirley Road for a couple of pints before they left. For some, this was "working a beat". In contrast, there were plenty of diligent, committed constables who really made a real difference to their communities. One organised a collection of toys for children every Christmas, and others took a personal as well as professional interest in the lives of people on their beat they had known for years.

There were, though, always officers in any department who did not see their main job as being in the police: it was merely a way of being paid a regular amount each month while they used every other opportunity to make money or conduct activities in police time that were to their personal benefit. (From this description, it must have only been a deficiency in the ability to raise the required deposit that prevented some from standing for parliament.)

One officer, with a face like a Mexican bandit on a wanted poster, had a football pool round which, when it coincided with being on duty, simply used a job car to collect from his congregation. Neither rape nor robbery nor indeed race riots (unless the roads were heavily barricaded and probably burning) would thwart his collection.

As mentioned, a further benefit of ABO work was not working nights. Research indicated nights were not particularly good for longevity for those over forty. It certainly seemed to pay dividends for PC Percy Doolittle, who appeared to be in his eighties and looked older than Private Godfrey in Dad's Army. Beat work may have indeed taken its toll, as he was barely fifty.

Percy, although milder-mannered than a dozing dodo, simply refused to recognise the existence of probationary constables. No matter how often you acknowledged him or greeted him with a warm hello, he just blanked you. In his eyes, you were as if nothing: an embryo, a not completely formed being, an apprentice not worthy of his recognition. I suspected it was likely that he had been subjected to similar treatment as a new officer when he joined, and saw it as a kind of rite of passage. Similar behaviour existed in many blue-collar industries where there were apprentices. It was probationary status that was the issue. It wasn't personal. I saw him act very genially with anyone who had passed through the two-year barrier. I also discovered he took great pride in his work, acting discreetly to maintain a commendable serenity on his beat among a community he knew widely and deeply. Often ribbed for his surname, he did more than many in his mild, low-key way.

Dorothy Downton was also an ABO. She had originally joined the local city force as part of the women's policing department. In the 1960s, Women Police Constables (WPCs as opposed to the gender-neutral PC of today) were specifically recruited to be deployed on matters relating to children, lost and found property, and work not defined as "men's work", whatever that was exactly. Dorothy had enjoyed that job and had no interest whatsoever in the Equal Opportunities Act of 1974, which equalised her pay and work responsibilities. She had not joined the service to patrol the unruly parishes of Southampton in the dead of night or deal with some disputatious drunk. She would often lament about the days when she had done the job she had joined to do. Fortunately for her, she landed an area beat role in a respectable, if now shabby and faded neighbourhood surrounding Howard Road.

Many of the houses on her beat had belonged to the wealthy and lined wide avenues and crescents. Some were semi-mansions, with servants' quarters that led to the kitchen via a back staircase. It was this grandeur that was to be the area's downfall. The homes were too large and expensive to upkeep, and so were split into flats and bedsits. One morning, I called at one such house with Dorothy. It was still occupied by just one elderly lady, now in her eighties. Regretfully, she told us of the days of the fine horses and carriages that had travelled by outside her home and of the genteel families who lived there in both the pre- and post-First World War periods. She recounted the lovely pace of a refined existence now long gone, held now only in the memories of the few remaining, like her. She had not moved and, having stayed put, was witness to a descent that had seemed like the decline of a civilisation. I couldn't help but feel her sorrow as she related her emotion-laden tale of Christmases long past.

Dorothy was a dignified, kindly lady whom the male officers would apologise to if their language got overly industrial. She had quite a dry sense of humour, and on one occasion when I was fulminating in the parade room, complaining about this boss and that sergeant, she looked up over the top of her dainty spectacles and, rouged cheeks drawn in observed; "Brian, I get the impression that despite your bolshie behaviour, you'll do exactly as you're told to do, when you're told to do it, like a good boy." And she was, of course, absolutely right.

There were other characters in the ranks of the ABOs. Thumper Owen was a Rhyl-born rugby player with a Hampshire accent who found it less difficult to play the man than the ball. Well-intentioned, he could feel right from wrong and acted accordingly. Thumper wore his sporting and work injuries like medals. With his nose broken repeatedly and cauliflower ears from abrasive scrums, he had a face like a Rhondda rugby pitch in need of re-surfacing.

One morning, the ABOs were convened for a parade. This didn't happen regularly, but sometimes their sergeant wanted to get them all together to brief them and to try and instill a bit of team spirit and group identity. It would be twelve years or so before the release of Jurassic Park, but all present could have reasonably submitted themselves as extras, and I don't mean in human roles. The combined age around the parade room table would have, combined, been enough to stretch back in time sufficiently to warn King Harold to visit Haslemere rather than Hastings.

The ABO sergeant, Len Stoves, was an ex-detective and former training sergeant with a capacity for humour as large as his capacity for whiskey. As they sat, about to start the parade, Thumper was inappropriately dressed with his collar undone and his tie lying on the table. Everyone else was properly presented in uniform, if a little scruffily in one or two cases. (One officer looked like he spent his days picking over the refuse at the local authority tip.)

"PC Owen, uniformity if you please; this is a formal parade for duty: put your tie on," commanded the supervisor wearily. Everyone looked at the errant beatman. Just as he was about to pick up his tie to clip it on, Stoves changed his mind.

"Actually, no, don't put your tie on. All the rest of you, pull your ears out like this (he grabbed a lug and extended it like a giant pancake) and flatten your noses." He pushed his nose to the side, giving a good impression of Joe Bugner or Thumper Owen, take your pick.

Well, it was uniform. They had a laugh at times; I'll give them that.

15 Accidents Don't Happen?

Every probationer wants to drive a police car. If they don't, then they have clearly decided that they'd rather not do too much work during the duration of their police service. One or two crafty individuals did exactly that, completing their probation and moving directly to an area beat on the grounds that they "loved talking to people". What they didn't add was "as an alternative to working".

In the seventies, probationers at some stations were able to drive police cars very early in service. Around 1980, with police numbers boosted, Hampshire officers could expect to do a minimum of a year walking the beat before being eligible for "improver driving training". These courses had to be applied for, and there was, naturally enough, a waiting list.

The rationale of the course, other than to create a barrier to the effective deployment of resources, was to ensure officers had certain driving habits and standards before they were allowed to drive marked police vehicles in sight of the general public. Naturally, we had all passed a Department of Transport driving test, and most probationers had more powerful cars than those frugal 1.1-litre Ford Escorts supplied by the constabulary. Some forces, like Dorset, just took you out for a drive, and if you were competent, you were good to go. Not in Hampshire. Even if it caused logistical problems, driving a police car without your authorisation pass was absolutely forbidden.

The course lasted two weeks, during which time students were taught the "system" of police driving. A standout feature of this was to never cross your arms; you had to "feed" the steering wheel, which meant shuffling, really fast at times, from left to right or vice versa. I presumed this was a hangover from the 1930s, when steering was perhaps less precise, and steering wheels were the size of those wheels found on wagons heading to Tombstone, Arizona.

A gear change technique called "double declutching" was also taught; supposedly to create a smooth transition between changes. This might have been desirable in a racing car occupied by Stirling Moss, but it was of arguable value in a modern car with synchromesh gearing. It did, however, add additional complexity for students and kept driving school instructors in work.

How much you were actually taught depended on your instructor. One used the lessons as a personal shopping expedition, requiring students to pull in here or stop there so he could load the boot with bags of assorted shopping, pot plants and, at times, building materials. These students weren't so good at fast driving, but they were brilliant at parking.

Another instructor was more focused on the actual mechanics of teaching, although he had an odd training aid: a short piece of black rubber pipe. If you didn't know what it was for to start with, you soon did, as he'd hit you with it if you did something contrary to instruction. He continued doing this form of aversion therapy for many years until he came up against an ex-serviceman who made it clear that if he touched him, he'd shove the training aid into a place where something considerably longer than the arm of the law would be required to retrieve it. After that, the instructor's pedagogical technique modernised somewhat.

Despite the shop stops and physical assaults, the courses were sought after. Driving permits were prized, and no one wanted to lose one. Suspension was pretty much automatic if you had an accident or were involved in an "incident", as, according to several traffic department and regional training instructors, "accidents don't happen". Just ask Ted Kennedy.

In April 1982, Rick Radweldt was not long out of his probation. He was an affable, solidly built Winchester lad with a penchant for carbohydrates. Steady and sensible, he lived with his parents. He was a bit dour; a combination of being the only probationer on the shift before me and the fact that he was still carrying Manchester United's cup final defeats of 1976 and '79 for rather longer than was good for him. One late afternoon, Rick was acting as my taxi driver as I conducted an enquiry in Millbrook. He hadn't long had his driving authorisation.

I was intending to give the outcome of a theft of a pedal cycle investigation to a rather attractive young medical student. As no investigation could be done, the visit was purely PR. Usually, we wouldn't bother with giving updates on petty crimes, but she was a trainee medic with a big smile, and I did have the idea of asking her out with the killer chat-up line that I was considering buying a tandem.

My courage deserted me on the doorstep, and I wanted to go like a diner with dysentery, but it didn't matter, as she wasn't in. Slightly dejected, I walked back to the car in the warmth of the late afternoon sunshine, and we drove off along the main route through the estate, past innumerable identical houses towards a large tower block on our right. At this juncture, we got a call to attend a chip pan fire. Ever hopeful of making a heroic life-saving intervention in a blazing building, or perhaps just pulled by the call of chips, Rick stated, "That's a blue lighter," and accelerated, flicking the switch to illuminate the patrol car's roof light.

As we gained momentum, the car in front of us indicated right and pulled out around a parked truck. It was going rather slowly, so Rick decided to overtake. This would have been all right if the driver hadn't been signalling a right turn at the next junction.

At one-third of the way along the offside of the car, the driver decided to execute the turn he had indicated. We were doing thirty miles an hour (your honour, on my baby's life). We hit the turning car on its rear driver's side. I'd never been involved in a collision with another car before. The bang of the impact was loud. I was surprised that, despite us not travelling particularly fast, the collision caused the pristine BMW 3 series to spin uncontrollably around and around like a machine-gunned Messerschmitt in terminal flight.

The Beamer rotated, now like a Vietnam helicopter in big trouble, bouncing up and over the curb and flying across a wide, and fortunately empty, expanse of grass. It stopped by colliding with a road nameplate, snapping it off with great force and catapulting it into the air. The car came to rest in an adjacent hedge on the street corner.

The white Ford Escort with POLICE written down the side in bold letters was now stationary in the centre of the junction. I got out and looked at the sorrowful front end. It was V-shaped; the radiator split and leaking like a burst bladder. The weakly rotating blue light on the roof, suggesting it was still "game on", was at odds with the car's terminal diagnosis.

The driver of the BMW marched over, visibly upset. "I thought you guys were trained to drive?" he exclaimed. Nice. Why bring me into it?

Actually, as I wasn't driving, my mood was significantly lighter than Rick's. He was digesting the realisation that his coveted driving ticket was in serious jeopardy and a retest, at the least, would be an absolute certainty. Chirpily, some may judge even gleefully, I volunteered to call up to impart the good news to all and sundry on the radio. Rick, however, demonstrated greater maturity than I and decided that this particular death message should be his responsibility. He notified the patrol sergeant of the PVA[31], requesting his attendance with due solemnity, a heavy heart, and as much self-possession as he could muster in the circumstances.

The noise had attracted a reasonably sized crowd, and I explained to some curious onlookers what had occurred. It wasn't too difficult for them to work out. There presumably wasn't much on television that evening, given that one large family decided to relocate the kitchen table to the front garden close to the crash

---

[31] PVA: Police Vehicle Accident,

site, where they proceeded to eat their tea while watching the live entertainment. It was circus time, and I was trying not to be misidentified as the clown, mainly by staying on the passenger side. My success was only partial: at least I wasn't Coco playing the leading role.

Eventually, the sergeant arrived. Sergeant Pat Punker, a former traffic motorcyclist, was very adept at dealing with accidents and proceeded about his business with a benevolent, professionally dispassionate sternness, mindful of the disgruntled driver whose car was hidden in the hedge, like a partially disguised Panzer tank. As the sun fell behind the tower block, it got very chilly, and yet again, I regretted not placing a jumper between my tunic and shirt, as I started shivering.

Chalk marks were made on the road as the scene was measured and recorded. A recovery truck arrived like a zoological undertaker to remove the deceased panda. As was usual in cases like this, the actual "shout" we were going to was a non-event and certainly not worth the expense or risk. Luckily for Rick, he had bought a new pair of Dr Martin's boots recently, which proved useful because, in the next few months, he got quite a lot of wear out of them.

This didn't prove to be a particularly great time for Rick. He had applied for a position of inspector in the Royal Hong Kong Police. He had A-levels, was out of probation, and they took direct entrants from UK forces at inspector rank after completion of several months of training at the HK police college. The big day came, and Rick caught the train for his interview in the capital. Coming from a county force, albeit a large one, the first question he was asked on his board was, "Why didn't you join the Metropolitan Police and work in London?"

Rick's spontaneous reply of, "I don't like cities," was, in retrospect, a tad ill-advised. The interview did not last long after that.

I had managed to get to the latter part of 1982. Just a few more weeks and I am, as they say in the Mafia, a made guy. But until then, I'm not.

I had one attachment to complete: two weeks in the traffic department (these days called roads policing). Given my innate lack of coordination (I could walk the beat but couldn't keep one on a drum) and my rather average driving ability, I didn't really see a future in this branch, although there were things to learn, as I was about to discover.

I arrived for an early turn start of 6 a.m. with my allotted shift at their base at Eastleigh Traffic, call-sign Lima Mike. It was a small building in the yard of Eastleigh Police Station.

It was my job, of course, to wait on the old sweats around the table, and I produced a brew and then sat down. There was me, four PCs, and the traffic sergeant, Perry Hawthorne. The surname was apt, as he could be a bit prickly. His nickname among the troops was "Merry" because, well, generally, he wasn't.

Quizzically, Merry looked at me.

"What did you do before you joined?"

"Student sarge." (A slight corruption of the facts, but it sounded way better than schoolboy.)

"Oh. Ever do any practical job?"

"Not really."

"Any jobs about the house?"

"A few."

"Clean any windows, did you?"

"Sometimes."

"Use any tools to do this at all, perhaps?"

"A bucket, I guess."

"How about a ladder?"

"Yeah, we had a ladder."

"OK. This ladder. Do you still have access to it by any chance?"

"Well, not really, not here, I suppose... maybe, why?"

"Just asking."

"Why do I need a ladder?"

"Well, it's just because maybe, if you could be so kind as to go and get it for me, I CAN USE IT TO GET DOWN TO DRINK MY FUCKING TEA!"

I looked at the container of liquid in front of him, noticing there was a discernible drop from the lip of the mug down to the surface of the PG Tips below. "No chance of it spilling, though," I added, but half wished I hadn't, given the look on his face.

As it happens, his little routine made me shake with laughter: I could only hope it was meant to be funny. He certainly possessed an acidic sense of humour, but then you could understand why when you appreciated what these officers dealt with: more death than CID by a long way, and the sergeants attended every one.

The PCs around the table seemed to enjoy the light entertainment. All were long-serving constables, and it's just as well they had cars to get around in, as at least two looked like they were unable to walk the length of themselves. I spent a few days with a couple of benign chaps that mainly involved cruising at various speeds, some very high (to maintain their driving standard, apparently), on the

M27. In between times, we would call in at Romsey police station just in time for morning or afternoon tea. The most demanding experience was trying to park the Jaguar in the very narrow rear yard of the station. It was all frightfully civilised. I don't remember doing any police work, though.

Control room tasking relating to routine criminal matters was avoided. Sometimes, road traffic accidents were reluctantly accepted unless it was an injury accident, and then it seemed everyone lit up with a vigorous sense of duty, and off we would all go. On day one, I did nothing more than a very thorough wash and wax of the Jaguar and a Range Rover, which had a telescopic floodlight on the roof. They had slave labour and intended to use it to the full. As part of my car wash work experience, I was introduced to the use of newspaper to clean car windows and found that, with a bit of elbow grease, it worked very well.

After a fairly tedious first week, where I was introduced to the complexities of tachographs and had a brain freeze as a result, things hotted up. On a 6-2-night shift, a large disturbance in Ringwood required units to attend from the city, twenty or so miles away. It was close to home territory near Ferndown, so I was keen to attend. My Range Rover driver, a ginger-haired Scot dubbed "Rob Roy" (Rob Roy of the Range Rover tonight), was less enthusiastic. However, I convinced him I knew the town. In reality, this meant I'd been to a few pubs there and could identify the caravan where "The Dutchman" provided fried takeaway food from the Netherlands, all served with the novelty of mayonnaise.

Force Control Room called to stand us down. However, as we were on the dual carriageway at full throttle, Rob assured them our presence would be useful as we had "local knowledge on board." That would be me, then. As we got to the outskirts of Ringwood, he asked me where the police station was. It was at this point that I started to feel uncomfortable, as I had no idea. As I prevaricated, he became less than impressed. Thinking less on my feet and more from my seat, I concluded that if it wasn't in the places I knew, it must be in a place I didn't know. Einstein would have been proud of me, possibly Sherlock as well. I directed him, with false confidence, in the direction of Christchurch Road, where I was rewarded with a blue lamp sticking out from a white building around which a large number of youths were milling. They had initially come to petition for the release of some of their comrades, but now it seemed they were more interested in consuming the chips and cheesy products they had bought from the Hook of Holland's greatest, and possibly only, export to The New Forest.

A thin, greying sergeant with a somewhat wolverine countenance thanked us for coming. He only had three PCs on duty, so any cavalry from anywhere was greatly received. A Dorset unit had also pulled up in a spirit of cross-border cooperation. It was a nice gesture, as they tended to be as scarce as hen's teeth. Hearsay had it that locals in one part of that county had put up posters bearing the question, "Have you seen this man?" Underneath was a picture of a Dorset bobby[32].

With the disturbance calmed, there followed a slower and silent return to Southampton across the darkly desolate forest. We returned to base to do paperwork and eat. By now, it was around 1 a.m. I had barely chewed through an unappealing cheese and onion sandwich before we were called out again by a controller with real urgency in his voice. Another matter that was non-traffic related but very serious: a householder fighting with an intruder.

We scrambled like fighter pilots, blue light reverberating off rapidly passed buildings. There were three of us this time: one of the guys doing an early morning car clean was driving. We screamed into long, respectable, and residential Hiltingbury Road to see the Eastleigh area car racing towards us from the other end, its headlights flashing and blue light bouncing off of trees and houses. Our main beam picked out a cluster of people outside a bungalow.

A middle-aged woman and her teenage daughter were standing, huddled and shivering, more with fear than cold, as their rotund and balding pyjama-clad man of the house wrestled breathlessly on the front lawn with a youth sporting a hairstyle like the spine of a dinosaur. Clad in safety pins and tartan, he was some variant of a "punk rocker". At this point, the youth was winning - but not for long.

For the second time tonight, we played the role of the Seventh Cavalry, but this time in a seriously significant way. The two patrol cars pulled up almost together: the area car in the street, with our BMW breaking to an abrupt, gravel-churning standstill on the driveway. The scene was awash with the swirl of strobing light as five officers exploded from their cars and leapt upon the punk (making the not unreasonable conclusion he was the culprit).

Sid Vicious the second was quickly removed to our car, resisting, spitting, and mumbling about, "The glue, the glue." From his sallowness and the red rash around his nose and mouth, sniffing is what he has been doing, with the break-in probably motivated by an urge to fund more. My first assessment was, he might not be pretty, but he did appear to be pretty vacant. I got in the car, and he was placed beside me, where he immediately dropped his head, intent on biting my

---

[32] Around this time Dorset has more crime than Surrey but around 400 fewer officers. Its force strength was a little under 1200: a third of Hampshire's.

thigh. He would have, too, had it not been for the quick reactions of Roy of the Range Rover, who grabbed him just in time and threatened to put a nerve hold on him. I didn't know what that was, but it sounded as painful as it was impressive. Sid, it seemed, was similarly impressed as he became a bit more docile. This, though, might have been more to do with him being handcuffed and having a firm grip placed on the spinal column on his head. He continued to mutter in a deluded tone as I kept a close eye on his teeth.

It's not hard to understand the feelings of utter relief and rescue that family felt at our rapid and decisive intervention. Their tears, let alone words of gratitude, said it all. This is what the public wants the police for, and it's what the police want to do. We all went home very satisfied that night. Well, all except Sid. He wasn't going anywhere.

There's no shortage of Post-Traumatic Stress Disorder among traffic officers. They get an overdose of sudden, brutal, horrific death, seeing multiple fatalities cutting across age groups. The officers who are road death investigators attend even more scenes, as do the supervisors who are required to attend by policy. It's often those who appear toughest on the outside who are suffering most on the inside. Detectives might often get the glory, but when it comes to sudden violent death, traffic officers are in a league of their own.

There had been a fatal accident on the Bitterne Road. The commuter traffic was backed up, and the scene coned off. Several traffic units were in attendance. Traffic investigators were present, including one who was tall and darkly curly-haired with a shrill voice. As he seemed to border on organised chaos, I nicknamed him in my head "Mayhem". Actually, he was a very professional, caring, and popular officer. When he wasn't at work, and often when he was, he grafted tirelessly for the sports and social club, organising the children's Christmas parties and playing Santa every year.

At an injury accident scene a few days before, Mayhem had pointed out a tyre track that indicated a car had left the road, mounted the kerb, driven a few meters along the verge and onto the footpath where, unsurprisingly, it had met resistance from a pedestrian who had ended up and over an adjacent garden wall. A factory worker coming home off nights had been intending to get into a bed, just not one containing marigolds, magnolias, and horse manure. Fortunately, his injuries were slight. The plants, though, took a bashing. Showing me the tyre tracks leading from the grass back to the road surface, Mayhem asked me what I noticed. I looked hard, but other than a tyre track, I couldn't see anything remotely revealing. "Look again," he prompted. I looked really, really hard. Nothing. "Can you see a tyre tread mark?" he asked encouragingly.

"Yes," I replied slowly, failing to grasp what he was getting at. Concluding that I was unlikely to ever make Baker Street my home address, he assisted my deductive process.

"If you can see a tread mark, then that means the wheel was still turning." The penny dropped.

"Ah, you mean the driver never braked?"

"Exactly. We'll make an accident investigator out of you yet."

On the Bitterne dual carriageway, at the scene of the fatal accident, Mayhem wanted to take measurements to record the position of vehicles at the scene, using fixed points as his reference. I was deployed, wearing a spare oversized traffic cap, which made me look like a whippet racer from Whitby. In my hands, I had a large orange tape measure and was directed to walk backwards along the carriageway. As I did so, a high-pitched voice cried out, "Mind the claret!"

I glanced behind me and saw a large patch of wine-coloured liquid closing in about my boots. The body had gone, but the residue still remained. Soon, sand would be spread like sawdust in a butcher's shop. It was brutal.

I counted myself fortunate that I never saw a road traffic death victim. The tales recounted by those officers who had seen many confirmed they would not escape the dark, indelibly printed memories. It's the suddenness, randomness, and horror of these deaths that shock and leave their mark. Other deaths are unpleasant for sure, but these are different. They linger in a different way. Hats off to the traffic cops who choose to deal with this carnage. I handed my oversized white topped cap back with appropriate respect. My traffic attachment was over.

16 Football Duty

Aged thirteen, I visited a small car panel-producing factory in Aston, West Midlands, as part of a school trip to the "Black Country". (A female teacher strongly objected to the use of this term because it was racially insulting. It had to be explained to her that the term's origin had to do with the dirt of the industrial age. It being 1974, nobody questioned her perceptions of the ethnic makeup of the region, given it was predominantly white.)

Having visited the home of Wedgewood pottery and then seen glass blowing in a factory warmer than the surface of a tin roof in Timbuktu, I found myself in a back street, on the shop floor of a small industrial unit, quite horrified at the conditions before me. I was confronted with noise, harshness, and repetition. A man pulled down a press every few seconds as a conveyor belt put another piece of metal to be shaped in front of him. Working hours were eight to four with a half hour for lunch. A handwritten notice set out tea break times and how they were to be strictly adhered to. For some people, this was their life: their life's work. It was shocking. It made me realise the importance of education. I promised myself there and then to pay more attention in arithmetic and concentrate more on chemistry - anything to escape this hell on earth, which, very arguably, signified the high point of our development as a modern industrial civilisation.

I remember thinking that I now knew why some Aston Villa supporters screamed, shouted, and scrapped on a Saturday afternoon. Who wouldn't want to get off their face for a couple of hours and drink themselves into oblivion when confronted with the impending Monday morning return to the industrial frontline? And, of course, when I policed football, I *tried* to have this in mind. Still, it didn't justify fans acting like thugs or vile racists.

Talking of racists, in my mind's eye, I'm standing in The Dell, Southampton FC's ground, near the West Stand and Milton Road end, looking down to the caged-in away supporters at the Archers Road. It was like looking at an exhibit at a Victorian zoo, with the animals behind grey-painted bars. This, of course, was the issue; supporter safety wasn't the priority. Controlling the warring factions by using enclosures was. Of course, we all know the awful fallout from these short-sighted control methods that prevented overspill onto the pitch in an emergency.

It didn't help that some supporters did their best to behave like animals. Maybe the cages encouraged them. Behind the bars, where he perhaps belonged, I saw a figure I term, with no affection whatsoever, as "Reg the Racist".

You couldn't discern this by his shortness of stature, his thick, black-framed glasses, or his trainspotter's anorak. At that point, he resembled an academic from Canterbury. No, it was demonstrated by his behaviour. Reg felt the best way to prove his white racial superiority was to jump up and down like a three-year-old having a tantrum. Additionally, with arms curved out at the sides like a gunslinger, he appeared to be trying to portray a representation of a chimpanzee that needed a prescription of Ritalin.

The stimulus for this lowbrow display of high-end immaturity was the approach of the brilliantly fast black Southampton winger. It was as comical as it was enraging. Every time the player exploded down the left wing with the ball towards the Archer's Road end, Reg would be triggered into action, bobbing about behind the bars as though on a bouncy castle. As the player receded like the tide at Weston shore, Reg would become docile and becalmed, only to spring up again like a jack-in-the-box at the slightest hint of the player becoming close enough to hear his infantile abuse.

I decided to pay Reg a personal visit in his playpen. I slipped out and around the ground into the Archers Road end through the heavy and guarded red gates. I then had to force my way down between the packed spectators to the front railings.

Reg was focused intently on his target, which helped me get up nice and cosy to mine. Standing directly behind him, I waited for my moment. It didn't take long. The ball swept out to the left, and the Saints attacked. As soon as the object of his hatred came into insult range, Reg was stimulated into a fit of high-octane animation. This time, Reg's repertoire comprised a combination of rapid chimp hopping on alternate feet, pretend banana peeling, and frantic mock munching.

It must have been this that upset his stomach and made him think he'd soiled his Levis. Or maybe it was my black-gloved hand planting itself firmly on his left shoulder. To be fair, it probably wasn't the hand on its own. Reg glanced around with what appeared to be indignation (possibly indigestion), which turned immediately to surprise. This gave way to terror when he looked up to see a less-than-impressed seven-foot copper glaring at him from under the brim of a helmet that itself was only marginally shorter than he was (before jumping).

For the benefit of his surrounding playmates, I placed a black finger under his snout and "told him his fortune," as we say in the trade, before leading him out by his hood for ejection from the ground. In an act of compassion, I let him visit the toilet first. It would have been out of paper by then, but maybe he found a discarded banana skin to wipe his arse with.

Football duties at "The Dell" were exciting and seen as a bit of a jolly by most officers who elected to work them. Probationers were allowed to volunteer after being signed off for independent patrol. As the club paid, they were performed on overtime after the early turn or on a rest day.

At my first ever match, I was allocated a duty which was regarded as a safe start, a position among the more docile supporters who were under the west stand. I was told by the older, sardonic PC I was with that this was the most challenging location in the ground, as you had to identify the players by their knees. I realised what he meant when, from the darkness at the back behind standing supporters, I discerned that the upper seated tier was so low it cut off the view across the pitch. About the midway point, the players' torsos vanished, leaving socks and patella patterning as the principal form of understanding who was who. The only real exception to this was the diminutive Southampton captain and footballing legend Alan Ball, who could still be identified by the number 7 on his shirt and his uniquely squeaky voice.

A small white building across Milton Road, next to a colourful burger van, was Dell Control: the police operational centre for matches. Here, an officer ran the radio channel used for the match, while others processed persons ejected from the ground. Arrested persons also came here to be held in a prison van pending transportation to the cell block. As with arrests on shift, junior officers took pride in getting ejections, generally for some repeated infractions like making obscene and insulting gestures to the opposition. Ejection was arguably more likely where these hand gestures obstructed the view of the game by the ever-watchful law.

On my first ejection, the surrounding crowd murmured in disbelief as I repeatedly said, "Excuse me", moving softly as I tried to ease my way between spectators. "The Gentle Touch" might have been on TV, but it had so far been absent from the terraces in more ways than one: women officers didn't seem to volunteer much for these duties, because they were not permitted to do so.

Although many officers were on three- or four-hour football duties, some were on a full-paid rest day. This was "a nice little earner", with a late start around ten, a free lunch provided, and a reasonable likelihood of watching the match.

One football duty, we were briefed by Superintendent Sicily, who told us that if he saw officers patrolling in groups of three or more, they would be "stuck on".

This meant being reported for a disciplinary offence. He was all heart, and if we saw him ambling down the road, we diverted anywhere, avoiding interaction with him like he had a venereal disease. This was a good policy because if he caught you doing something he didn't like, you'd be fucked. I'm sure he had a more pleasant, possibly even humorous, nature. Someone just needed to remind him to bring it to work occasionally.

Another time, an army of Birmingham City supporters got off the train. This was regrettable. Had they started drinking earlier, they might have missed us and got off in Bournemouth. Better still: Barcelona. These supporters were like an invading army, and in a tightly formed group of several hundred, they marched into the city centre, popping into the Tyrell and Green department store in Above Bar as they went. In through one double door and out another, they did a spot of clothes shopping en route, niftily bypassing the tills. One, carrying a particularly fetching scarf, was picked off by a couple of PCs and detained. The arresting officer was particularly livid as he was a former employee of the store and still popped in to catch up with his ex-colleagues, mainly the ones in the makeup and lingerie departments.

The mob, the likes of which led to the formation of the police in the first place in the 1820s, made for the Lord Louis pub by the Rose Gardens. Its leaders had seemingly done their research, as it was the top Saints supporter's stomping ground and packed with red-striped drinkers drinking Red Stripe. Pasteurised Pete wasn't in there as he was on duty.

Police intercepted the horde in the nick of time, and the rumbustious rabble was directed away like a runaway coal train that had its rails switched. Police led, the invasion force then embarked on a round Southampton city centre march that guided them indirectly towards the ground. They arrived early, but there were burger bars eager to feed them, and, like any army on the move, they were now hungry. Police tactics were that this was probably the best way to distract them. If their hands were filled with hot dogs and hot chocolate, they couldn't realistically steal anything or punch anyone. It didn't stop a couple from having a try, though.

During the game, the natives from the Midlands felt a lack of attention, leading to them acting out a kind of Zulu tribal dance in the East stand seats they had occupied in numbers. This seemed odd as, as far as I could see, they were all white. They seemed very proud of their efforts, and the locals gave them the recognition they craved via a slow hand clap of appreciation with a few "wanker" gestures thrown in, all in a spirit of family-friendly fun. It was a touching moment. Not.

It was a Saturday late shift. There was crowd trouble at Fratton Park, home of Portsmouth FC. The Blues were playing arch-enemies Cardiff City. Quite why there was animosity between the two, I didn't know. Robert Wrench did. "Battle of the second division ports," he asserted as a born and bred Sotonian.

Insufficient police resources had been allocated to the event, and the match commander wanted reinforcements. A police support unit (PSU: a van load of constables with a sergeant, sometimes two van loads including an inspector) was assembled from available staff in Southampton, and we were bused down the M27, sat on wooden bench seats in a Ford Transit prisoner van. I was apprehensive as I'd been led to believe the locals could be a bit feral on Portsea Island, and things must have been quite bad for us to be called in.

On arrival, some of the natives were certainly hostile. I'd been to a football match at Celtic Park in Glasgow around 1975. It was a summer friendly against Penarol, the South American champions. Other than seeing Kenny Dalglish slot in two marvellous goals, my abiding memory was seeing several people being led out with bloodied heads. This was a result of some anti-socials in the crowd tossing empty pocket-sized whisky bottles into the crowd, like fireworks at a fiesta. That was a friendly with no opposition supporters. Here we were led into a baying and pulsating theatre filled with venom, anger, and hate. At first, I thought it was directed at the opposition from over the Severn Estuary, but it seemed to be turning against us, the police, for the simple reason that we were obstructing the view.

We had been brought in to surround the pitch and face the crowd, creating a barrier to prevent a pitch(ed) battle—literally. The match was coming to its conclusion, and passions were running higher than a tap in Tibet. To show their displeasure, the locals in the North stand tossed coins at us. To start with, I didn't realise what the gesture meant. I couldn't see a wishing well, and certainly, the crowd was not wishing us well, even if they were wishing for a change of fortunes and another goal. I then saw someone with a cut cheek and realised what was up. At that point, for me, it was eyes down in the hope I wouldn't be hit. It was an uncomfortable experience. At the final whistle, which couldn't come quickly enough for me, the ground staff (some of whom looked like they were performing community service as an alternative to prison) collected the coins which had fallen, like confetti at a wedding. Somehow, I doubt they donated the proceeds to charity.

We then deployed in the narrow, congested terraced roads to the south of the ground to keep the rival factions apart as the "sheep shaggers" from across the

Severn, as the locals termed them, embarked on trains and coaches bound for the land of the leek. An engraved plate glass pub window was shattered as we shepherded frisky local youths (skinny, spotty individuals without work or girlfriends with which to discharge their energies) off into the back streets to disperse. We played cat and mouse with them for a while until the opposition fans had departed and the locals' reason for performing had gone. Finally, bored and hungry, they withdrew back to the security of their homes, mothers, apron strings, and their tea. Another football duty was at an end.

17 Public Order Training

The riots of Brixton, Toxteth and elsewhere across the country, with their pictures of bloodied police officers defending themselves with dustbin lids, had not played out well, and there was a comprehension in the upper echelons of the service, where strategic decisions are occasionally made, that effective equipment and training might now be required.

A few of us from the shift, with others drawn from around the force, found ourselves at the force training centre at Netley to be "public order trained". There was no purpose-built facility for this at the time, so exercises took place on the driveway in front of the Georgian-style white-stoned main building, to the surprised amusement of visitors, unless they were familiar with historical battle re-enactments.

We congregated in small groups, with a few inhaling on what would be a last cigarette for an hour at least. There was a golden-haired, angular, athletic chief inspector limbering on the spot; white rugby shirt collar turned up in the style of Jimmy Connors, the US tennis champ. Robert Wrench dubbed the V-shaped demigod "chief inspector torso"; as the would-be Olympian prepared for what he regarded as the serious business of running. (Regrettably, halfway around, like a finely tuned racehorse, he pulled a muscle and retired injured. Unlike an injured horse, he wasn't shot.)

A rather arrogant training sergeant, accurately described by one PC as "Gobby Gary Garside", took us for a warm-up jog that we quickly determined was an

Olympic qualification event in disguise. Garside was from Goole or some other northern outpost where men are allegedly men, and the merest hint of any trait that might be designated vaguely feminine, such as kindness, grace, or lack of toughness, was ruthlessly expunged from the errant male psyche.

As "Gobby" surveyed the bent-over, wheezing creatures gasping for breath in front of him, he observed, in a voice loud enough to be heard in Yorkshire, "Bloody hell, there must be some very dissatisfied wives in these parts."

"What a twat," observed Locryn Fox. There were murmurs of general agreement that this seemed a reasonable assessment of our instructor, if biologically inaccurate. This negative assessment was, though, fueled partially by jealousy at his ability to look athletic in his running bottoms and T-shirt. I'd seen more fat on a box of Special K.

We did some "orderly movement", a sort of half march designed to revive our dormant memories of drill instruction from training school. The memory had left the building in some officers as the movement was anything but orderly, with some PCs ambling off like cows slyly slipping out of line at an abattoir.

Files were formed between buildings as we practised cordons. Supervisors, generally unfamiliar with the hard command and control model as used by the military, had to find their inner sergeant major and project like they were in a Puccini at the Palladium.

We then did short shield training. These shields were round and reminiscent of both the dustbin lids of Brixton and the personal protective equipment of the ancient Britons. Fortunately, they didn't come with a flint axe. I did note, though, that the shields had been thoughtfully designed for right-handers only.

There were two handles on the inner surface, one wide and designed for the forearm, one shorter to be gripped by the hand. The disc has been configured for the word POLICE to display the correct way up—if you were right-handed. As a left-hander, I was identified as a deviant. This was at least historically consistent. To hold the shield comfortably, I needed to reverse it, displaying the word ECILOP. It looked slightly Cyrillic, and I took a guess that it meant "diversity" in Russian. Actually, I didn't. As stated previously, the term diversity hadn't been invented yet. Instead, I just had to live with it and be glad they hadn't tried to train me by tying my left hand behind my back, like in the Middle Ages—a time when these public order drills wouldn't have seemed out of place. I expected a forty-five-minute session on the tactics of Boadicea to follow shortly.

Gobby Gary didn't like the reversed letter look as it offended his sense of uniformity and rather simplistic worldview that everything should be equal in the eyes of the law. In this case, as he was the law, it's his eyes we're talking about. I visualised a peace activist trying to reason with Gobby. Then I got real and concluded that the activist would last about thirty seconds before being clubbed to extinction like a baby seal on a Canadian ice floe.

We spent some time fending off baton blows, like extras from Spartacus, before a tea break and the ominous long shields and petrol bomb exercise. The long shields were exactly that: a shield about five feet long capable of withstanding the inclination to melt if doused in petrol. We crouched down behind our respective shields, clinging to the double grab handles. Here, we established that being short was a great advantage, as some officers could almost stand up behind theirs, leaning against them in casual relaxation to the point they could almost have a crafty fag. For the more elongated, like me, we found ourselves tortured by having to bend at what was about a one-hundred-and-twenty-degree angle. I concluded that I could do this for about five minutes before a lower back muscle spasm attack and about ten minutes before I would need traction.

As an inducement to attend, we had been issued new NATO helmets. These were blue, had a visor and bore the word POLICE across the top. Crucially, they could be worn by both right and left-handers. Those who rode motorcycles were familiar with wearing this type of helmet. To those who preferred four wheels in contact with the ground at all times, there was a degree of claustrophobia and sensory deprivation that made one feel like a deep-sea diver.

We were formed into threes and instructed to create an interlocking super shield, with the edges of the two outer shields behind the one in the middle. The theory was that the outer shield carriers pushed, with the one in the middle, me, pulling, creating a lock. The Instruction, "pressure on", rang out but was received as a muffled utterance, like someone was talking to me while my head was underwater. We locked shields in our individual worlds, shuffling from side to side like cartoon crabs. The physical strain was significant and was only marginally preferable to sitting on a red-hot spike, where at least you'd be upright. Forming clusters of three super shields, we shuffled back and forth like we were performing a country dance. All that was missing was a hopping fiddler and some guy playing an accordion.

There was a flash and a surge of heat. I then noticed flames licking around the bottom of my shield where I had lifted it very slightly off the ground to move forward, contrary to the impossible-to-follow instructions. The front of the shield was flaming like an under-ready barbecue. I had taken a direct hit to the shield, that is, as opposed to the petrol bomb dropping over it and striking me. If it had, there were, unreassuringly, two somewhat indifferent individuals with fire extinguishers, inattentively chatting nearby, whose job was to nullify the overall severity of the burns and keep them respectably below third-degree.

As liquid fuel is more expensive than wooden blocks and less recyclable, the actual number of petrol bombs was few. However, they were delivered by other instructors who loved their job and had developed an unerring level of accuracy. The wooden bricks that were lobbed in a torrent were being delivered by the rent-a-crowd that comprised half of our training group. These defenders of the state were taking full advantage of their temporary role change and were acting with the enthusiasm of unbridled anti-capitalist marchers. The two teams, those participating as rioters and those participating as police, swapped after a break. The instructors had sneakily constructed the training day by drawing officers from Southampton and Portsmouth, two cities with an unnatural degree of antipathy to each other based on nothing more than the tribal stupidity of some of the people living or working there. This "groupthink" infects even the most sensible of individuals, and police officers. As a consequence, the ferocity of the attack we were subjected to was somewhat greater than we might have reasonably expected and only slightly less than that experienced at Rorke's Drift. (Exaggeration, but you get the point.)

After lunch, it was our turn to stand up straight. The essential characteristics of the two cities were demonstrated again, even though they had already been. Those of us from Southampton were a bit easier going and aware we were actually in a training environment with colleagues and that, as the thin blue line, we should remember this. The officers from Portsmouth, though, perhaps more highly strung, having to deal with local football supporters who at the time found the entertainment of fighting on the terraces infinitely preferable to the quality of football on display on the pitch, had engaged with a kind of fervour for battening that I had only ever seen on news reports from Paris involving the CRS.

The ability of normal people to transform into ugly personality types very quickly is well evidenced in psychology[33], and here we had more material to

---

[33] Stanford Prison Experiment 1971 where students played roles of prisoner and guard. The experiment had to be stopped early as the guards were getting a little too into the role.

substantiate these findings. One ultra-smart, "Peter Perfect"[34] looking PC seemed to have regressed to the Stone Age as he squatted, baton drawn and ready for battle, completely in the kill zone. If only we could have found him a sabre-toothed tiger. I'm sure he would have pummeled it to death, mistaking its markings for a Southampton supporter.

The day concluded with most of us realising we were out of condition: some massively. Mostly, though, the view was that the riots were passed, and this training had come rather too late. In reality, we were rehearsing, although we just didn't know it; the Thatcher-Scargill punch-up was waiting just around the corner.

Oh, and Sergeant Fox got his NATO helmet. Prudently, I decided to make no comment, even though there was no locker nearby.

18 (No) Angel Delight

The children's pudding of the 1970s, which tasted more chemical than a chlorine cocktail, wasn't the only distasteful angelic experience of that period. A group of bikers had formed in California in 1948 and, by 1966, were the subject of the film "Wild Angels", where they were shown as a violent criminal gang. Hunter S. Thompson published his book, "Hell's Angels", the same year, latching on to a group of bikers for twelve months or so, and getting a trip to hospital for his efforts after four decided he was exploiting them and gave him a bit of a kicking.

In 1979, an "unsanctioned chapter" from Windsor had been attacked by a group of thirty Angels while camping in the New Forest. The Windsor leader was shot three times in the head, while another got a rash known to some as "buckshot backside" after his biker's buttocks were peppered with pellets.

My knowledge of the group was only from popular culture, but it was clear they had a reputation for being violent and intimidating. This was an image they were happy to maintain. With their bikes, beards, badges, and black leathers, they

---

[34] Wacky Races 1968-70 TV cartoon character.

resembled motorised Vikings; exhibiting, at the very least, a general attitude of lawlessness that was unsettling to the onlooker.

My first local exposure to them was when I was driven past a rather run-down and nondescript address way down the bottom of Shirley Road. I was told how a search of the small house, or more accurately, hovel, had led to the discovery of a revolver. I think the PC who told me was trying to impress me. If that was his intention, he certainly succeeded. Guns were pretty much unheard of at this time in criminality, and very seldom encountered by the police. The good news was that the house had been vacated, and the local chapter had moved to another part of the city covered by central, so they were no longer our immediate problem.

The new Chapter House was allegedly fortified with a steel door and nigh on impregnable; presumably a security upgrade in response to the search that had found the gun. It was supposedly a centre of drug supply and other nefarious deeds. At this time, local drugs comprised weed (cannabis) and amphetamine. Heroin and cocaine were not on the radar. The Angels were reputedly at the centre of operations regarding "amphet" (amphetamine), as it was called, and a number of other criminal enterprises. The Chapter House was located in an end terrace, with the chapter crest painted on the outside wall, like a mural from West Belfast, and was observable from the safety of a passing mainline train carriage. Whether fact matched the rumour, I don't know. They had certainly relocated to what was then known as the vice area of the city, and I presumed not just because rents were lower or it was more convenient for popping out for a quick shag.

In Shirley, we had another house which reputedly contained a group of "Angels". Certainly, they were bikers, as the posse of low-riding, high-handle-barred bikes parked outside seemed to testify.

The square, "White House" as we called it (in homage to Richard Nixon and the number of criminals it contained), sat alone in a side street at the dock end of town. It had a vacant, overgrown plot on one side and a large gravel area for parking immediately beside the kerb. There were usually around half a dozen bikes outside. For some reason, I barely ever saw anyone come or go into the house.

On a crisp, cold, clear night, around ten thirty, early in the week, I found myself walking slowly and dutifully down Park Road towards the Presidential Palace. Outside were several of the group's motorcycles. Harley-Davidson's, mainly, they were corralled, as if waiting for branding (or possibly re-branding). I could see a light glowing dimly in the front room.

My breath was condensing in the cold air, and the moonlight glinted on my helmet plate and tunic lapel badges, making me appear like a latter-day Praetorian Guard (to my mind, anyway). As I approached, I saw a flash of very bright light. It came from a large window on the west wing of the White House. I realised, in my squint-eyed curiosity, that someone was peering between the slats of a venetian blind and that the very bright light was blazing behind them like a searchlight at a penal colony.

As I advanced, gazing at the light in my measured, dignified, police-like manner, I was met by what I presumed was the best I was going to get in terms of a warm, congenial greeting from the angelic residents within.

"Fuck off, you nosey c**t," came a voice ringing out in the empty night, amplifying through the silence like a gunshot.

I glanced over my left shoulder, then right, and seeing that there was nobody in the vicinity, concluded that, yes, they must have meant me. With pride somewhat dented, while trying to suppress my laughter, I continued a slow patrol past, ensuring I made it clear I was examining licence plates as I did so, partly for its mildly harassing effect but mainly as an emollient to my pride. I didn't linger too long.

My next encounter, a few weeks later, involved a group of Angels in a van being stop-checked by two officers, PS Fox and a freckled Aberdonian PC called Hamish Pyle, around eleven at night outside a BMW dealership called Quadrifoglio. I was the observer in the area car. We had witnessed this group being spoken to as we drove past a few moments earlier. The next thing we heard was a frantic emergency assistance call for all units to respond.

My chauffeur, Donald, commented tersely that we should have parked up nearby and watched over our brothers in blue. He immediately put his foot down, driving into a right-hand bend, blue lights now flashing. In his heavy-booted enthusiasm, the backend of the patrol car broke away to the left, and the next second, we were pirouetting like ice dancers Torvill and Dean, but without the grace, elegance, or control. No gold medal was going to be awarded for this piece of police driving as we skated on thin ice, or rather grass, as the patrol car mounted the pavement.

Fortuitously, we just cleared the end of a row of terraced houses, and onto the green, we revolved across a footpath and out onto the main Romsey Road. Remarkably, we were now facing in exactly the direction we wanted and cut a corner and about twenty seconds off our travelling time, and all without striking anything else. Hannu Mikkola would have been proud. Unfortunately, this wasn't a world championship rally event, and even more unfortunately, an instructor from the police driving school lived at the end of the terrace. Alerted to the noise of the car banging into the kerb, he peered from behind his curtains like a nosey neighbour to see us sailing serenely past the side of his home.

Being a sly bastard, he asked questions the next day about whether "we were alright". This essentially faux welfare enquiry contained malice aforethought, leading to an inspection of the car and the discovery of a slightly buckled nearside hubcap that had evidently clouted the kerb. The investigation led to Donald's subsequent driving suspension for six months, not only from driving but from *even being carried in a police vehicle*. This additional punishment came as a result of the iron rule of the Deputy Chief Constable, who was making the point that the driver should have reported the damage and was covering the possibility that he knew about it but had decided to ignore it. Harsh, but when they wanted to make a point, they made a point. Donald was despondent, having to walk the beat. He barely knew how. I'm sure I spotted him trying to double-declutch and change gear a couple of times as he shuffled slowly from pavement to road. It was painful to watch.

Back to the assistance call: we rushed to the scene, arriving with other units converging on the location. There was pandemonium as various members of the Angelic gang decided to disperse from the scene of the crime. An unshaven, dirty-jeaned individual ran across the forecourt of the garage, with me and a traffic officer in hot pursuit. Not long out of training school, I was a bit quicker than the traffic cop, who had the nickname "Pete the Pie Man" due to his love of pastry. That, as a hobby, allied to eight hours sat mainly in a BMW 5 series, didn't make for either a rapid exit from the car or much speed on doing so. Therefore, it was me who caught up with the black-bearded biker, grabbing him at the rear of the showroom by the car wash. From the smell of him, I wished he'd run through it.

As I gripped his arm, I shouted, "You're apprehended," which was probably a posher term than he or I might have expected to pop out of my mouth. If he didn't understand that, then the arm lock applied probably assisted his comprehension. With Pie Man's assistance, we walked back to the area car.

There were police vehicles and the inevitable pulsating blue lights everywhere as the group was rounded up like bandits on a bank job gone wrong in El Paso. It transpired that one of Satan's disciples had objected to the stop check, calling an officer "A jumped-up bald-headed twat", and things had deteriorated from there, with both cops being assaulted. A couple of colleagues later pointed out that, although hurtful, as a matter of pure accuracy, the description had *some* validity.

Back at Shirley, the station sergeant bemoaned not having taken the night off. Central's cells were full, so he had some work to do, booking in a few surly bikers, guarded by a large group of constables. There was a palpable undercurrent of hostility, tension and simmering violence in the air.

With most arrested people, even after a fight, a degree of cordiality can be achieved back at the station. This was seldom the case with anyone self-identifying as an Angel, especially if any of their compatriots were present. There was an ideological contempt for police, and it was demonstrated in every utterance and action. For those who might be more personally reasonable or amiable, they were forbidden to be in the presence of others from the gang.

As we took a breather, another "ten-ten" emergency assistance call went out. Donald and I launched into the area car, dashing between rows of parked cars and an oncoming truck at an almost reckless speed, making it four abreast in the narrow, turn-of-the-century terraced back street of Foundry Lane. I was sure we were going to collide and felt it was only my incredibly sharp intake of breath that sucked the sides of the patrol car in enough for us to squeeze through an impossible gap.

Racing to the White House, we were confronted by an open front door and the two assaulted officers, Fox and Pyle. They and a third, Robert Wrench, were rolling about in the hallway, trying to subdue the gang member who initiated the punch-up in the first place and who had managed to escape the scene. I launched into the building, and we applied cuffs and placed the somewhat bruised and battered biker in the car, his white T-shirt looking rather greyer and redder than when he started the night.

A few months later, this entire fiasco led to most of our shift making consecutive appearances at the local Crown Court, where the bikers were on trial for assault and public order offences. This resulted in my giving evidence for the first time in that venue. I was incredibly nervous, in fact, almost sick at the thought. Having been nervous introducing myself at training school and having ducked giving the course dinner address by just a couple of lucky marks, I didn't want a court outing in front of a judge and jury. As it was, the court was less imposing than it should have been. The old court was shut as a new one was being built, so we were located in a group of porta-cabins that more resembled a mobile blood donation unit.

Remembering the advice from training school of "answer yes or no, your Honour" (you are addressing the court, not the defence barrister asking the questions), I did just that. I had the consolation of being commended on the quality of my evidence—not by the judge, unfortunately, but by the court usher. Well, you've got to start somewhere.

My best moment was when I was asked by a tall, self-important barrister (there's only one variable applicable here) whether I was trained as a police officer to have a good memory. This fiction seemed to exist in some quarters, and I shook my head, saying I hadn't had any at all. He seemed surprised by this reply and pursued another line of questioning.

It transpired afterwards that he asked Sergeant Punker the same question. The sergeant affirmed this was the case; he had been trained to be extra observant. He was promptly asked the colour and shape of the clock in the foyer outside the court. The predictable answer, "I don't remember," somewhat crushed his credibility. The lawyer looked round at the jury triumphantly before delivering the killer kick, "There is no clock, sergeant."

This kind of ploy is a favourite of barristers in their quest to undermine the credibility of a witness, especially in a case involving identification. It doesn't help when the witness assists in their own downfall. My evidence proved helpful in securing convictions of three months imprisonment for the main protagonists. We left the court satisfied. The bigger and better gang had won, it seemed.

That night, I attended a "press showing" with some of my shift. A newly released film was being screened for the press so they could report on its virtues - it helped sell newspapers and cinema tickets. These showings were open to police officers, partners and police staff. (The practice is long gone. Maybe someone questioned the ethics? Or maybe it's just that the cinema is now a shopping centre.) Screenings were usually at 10.30 or 11 p.m. Never wishing to miss out on a freebie, officers would pop into the police club first (cheaper drinks). As a result, there was usually a reasonable level of merriment and emotion amongst the audience.

On this occasion, the movie showing was "Death Wish 2". The genre's popularity meant that, unusually, the entire auditorium was completely full. I'd been to one or two press showings before, but nothing on this scale. The movie was about a vigilante who hunts down and takes terminal revenge on a gang of hooligans who commit rape and murder (the crime has to fit the punishment, you know). Little did I realise how much dormant frustration with the criminal justice system a few pints of beer could release. As Charles Bronson took his violent retribution, whoops of joy and unbridled enthusiasm filled the hall, with several of the audience excitedly jumping up on their seats, where they bounced around deliriously, spilling their popcorn and beverages. The hand clapping for the violent vigilante was as enthusiastic as delegates at an assembly of the North Korean parliament. I was grateful no reporter from the national press was present: the story wouldn't have been the film.

A few weeks later, I found myself just around the corner from the White House on foot patrol. I was directed to an injury road traffic accident, just a few hundred meters from me. Striding briskly around the corner, I was met with a peculiar sight. A motorcyclist was lying on the tarmac, immobile. He was several meters in front of his motorcycle, which was standing bolt upright. Unusual, but on inspection, it was easy to see why: the bike was pinned against a parked car by the offside front corner of a blue Ford Cortina.

    I checked the motorcyclist and saw it was Viking Vic, the black beard from the forecourt. He was breathing but unconscious, so I dragged him into the recovery position and called for an ambulance. On speaking to the driver of the Cortina, a small rotund commercial traveller in his fifties called Barry, it transpired the guilty party was a pile of very orange and benign builder's sand that had been dumped in the road at the kerb side. Barry had to wait for an oncoming laundry van to pass the sand before he could pull out around it. Unfortunately, Vic the Viking had decided it was too nice a day for a long boat and had taken his BSA motorbike out for a spin and was heading home to Nixon's Manor (or maybe I should say Reagan's Ranch, as he was President).

    Riding very close to the back of the van, perhaps trying to collect his or someone else's laundry, Vic wasn't visible to Barry, who pulled out just as the van cleared him, and subsequently, Barry pinned our bearded barbarian's bike firmly against the now dented car opposite. This left the laws of physics to propel Vik (real name Kevin) through the air like he'd been shot from a circus cannon onto the road surface, where he now lay with only a cat's eye for company. Barry didn't think he should have looked and didn't think he should be reported for driving without due care and attention. I begged to differ on both points.

    A week later, I visited Kevin in hospital. His legs were supported and in plaster, but otherwise, he was sat up and at least conscious, which was an improvement. He had clearly resisted shaving. I told him we had, of course, met before and enquired if the hospital food was any better than in prison. He smiled and said it was. As a biker, he naturally wanted to discuss the injuries to his bike more than the injuries to himself. I told him our past mishaps were behind us. I was present as he was the injured party, for which he showed visible relief and thanks, and I got on with the business of taking a statement from him as a victim. We were friendly and cordial (there were no other Angels present), and he was actually a reasonably OK guy in the circumstances. That's just how the job goes sometimes.

The reality was, though, that several of the local Angels proceeded along the highway to hell to the company of Old Nick rather sooner than they might have intended. High-speed motorcycles and a reckless attitude to riding them, combined with alcohol or amphetamine, meant that more than a couple ended up in fatal accidents. One, while looking backwards, giving the finger to an elderly couple at 90 mph, forgot the age-old rule that if you are going at 90 and the vehicle in front is doing 40, it's effectively coming toward you at 50. As a result, he blazed into the back of a baker's van on his Kawasaki and, as they say in the traffic department's version of rhyming slang, he became "brown bread".

A few years later, I saw a female gang member I remembered. She had gone from motorcycle moll, princess of the pillion, to a bitter, drug and alcohol-ravaged benefits dependent, crippled by injuries from a crash that affected her walking. I was no fan, but I felt a tinge of compassion for her plight. She was only in her early thirties.

They burned brightly, and often fiercely, but seldom for long.

19 The End of the Beginning

Friday, 12th of November 1982. I was in full uniform at police headquarters for my confirmation of appointment. All those from the group who had joined with me were present. We had all made it. One was already talking about retirement, although, to be fair, he did have three years of pensionable military service to be added, so he only had twenty-five years to go. Not all of us would make it to a pension, though.

One would get promoted early in service before a driving incident took both his licence and warrant card. Another, the likeable northern ex-navy pilot, who coveted the area car role, which he modestly and inaccurately saw as just a case of exchanging one cockpit for another (with less challenging navigation), had a sadly premature end. A back injury sustained while bounding over a garden wall in pursuit of a burglar put paid to his career. The wall was five feet on one side with a nine-foot drop on the other, and glass-encrusted. He still got his man, though. Enrolling as a very late-life student, he ended up as an academic lawyer, lecturing nationally for police training as an expert on the Human Rights Act. As a bonus, he got a visiting academic post in New York and eventually retired as a law professor with a house abroad. He didn't see any of that coming. Neither did I spot his potential, as he splashed gravy over my shirt at Ashford by bombing his plate inaccurately with boiled potatoes (I could at least see why he gave up military flying). A couple of others chose to become career detectives. Another became an area-beat sergeant, a role that came complete with bicycle clips (and a bike), and finally, another had a big time falling out of love with the job, resigning for pastures new.

Me? Well, there were many more twists, turns and experiences to come. I survived thirty years and a bit. A career, mainly in the CID, ensued, with positions as Head of CID in Portsmouth and Western Hampshire, followed by a stint as a tutor at the National Police College at Bramshill[35].

To achieve the above, though, I had come through two tumultuous years that took me from school uniform to police uniform. From school gate to prison gate. (Arriving at Send Youth Offenders Centre with a seventeen-year-old, the guard

---

[35] A stately home in north Hampshire, like so many police premises—Hulse Road, Shirley Police Station—was sold off for development, closing in 2015.

instructed, "On the double!" and, not long out of an institution myself, I found myself jogging with the prisoner in confused unison, like I was auditioning ten years early for The Shawshank Redemption.)

At times, I'd been exposed to the harsh realities of life (and death), all the while working with comrades who filled every day with humour, along with a true sense of camaraderie and vocation. None of us saw it as just a job: it was a way of life—a vocation—and it proved to be an incredibly rewarding experience. Little could I have realised what and how much was in store for me before passing that fateful medical.

The confirmation should have been with the chief constable, but he was away, apparently (an impudent whisper had it he was on a brewery trip, as he was known for having an affection for ale). The deputy was also absent, so it was left to one of the assistant chief officers to give us a brief pep talk to set us up for the remaining twenty-eight years of our service (with the exception of the one prospective retiree who, even then, was looking slightly smug).

The address was disappointingly low-key to the point that I can't remember it. As I left the toweringly imposing HQ building into the cool November air, sunshine streaming through the greenery of the tall trees in the lush grounds at West Hill, Winchester, I preferred to remember the words of the retired and formidable Chief Constable of Dorset, Arthur Hambleton. A former Royal Marines Major, he left his force pretty much as I was joining mine. I remember seeing a photograph of him looking uncompromisingly determined in Dorset Police's internal newspaper. His rather inspirational departing words were: "Remember. Do what is right and fear no man."

Yes, that'll do for me perfectly. Thank you, Arthur.

Dear reader! I hope you enjoyed these tales. *If you did, great! A request —if you liked them, please do share your experience with friends across social media by distributing any links, or by sending a photo of the cover.* **And, of course, reviews— particularly on Amazon—work wonders.** *For those of you who have had like experiences or amusing contact with policing in this time or any other, it would be great to read how this account may have resonated with your experiences.*

With very best wishes

Brian Mitchell

Autumn 2024

Printed in Dunstable, United Kingdom

76107509R00099